*Understanding Costs and Outcomes
in Child Welfare Services*

Child Welfare Outcomes
Series Editor: Harriet Ward, Centre for Child and Family Research, Loughborough University, UK
This authoritative series draws from original research and current policy debates to help social work managers, policy makers and researchers to understand and improve the outcomes of services for children and young people in need. Taking an evidence-based approach, these books include children's experiences and analysis of costs and effectiveness in their assessment of interventions, and provide guidance on how to develop more effective policy, practice, and training.

other books in the series

Improving Outcomes for Children and Families
Finding and Using International Evidence
Edited by Anthony N. Maluccio, Cinzia Canali, Tiziano Vecchiato,
Anita Lightburn, Jane Aldgate and Wendy Rose
Foreword by James K. Whittaker
ISBN 978 1 84905 819 3

How Does Foster Care Work?
International Evidence on Outcomes
Edited by Elizabeth Fernandez and Richard P. Barth
Foreword by James K. Whittaker
ISBN 978 1 84905 812 4

Costs and Consequences of Placing Children in Care
Harriet Ward, Lisa Holmes and Jean Soper
ISBN 978 1 84310 273 1

Young People's Transitions from Care to Adulthood
International Research and Practice
Edited by Mike Stein and Emily R. Munro
ISBN 978 1 84310 610 4

Babies and Young Children in Care
Life Pathways, Decision-making and Practice
Harriet Ward, Emily R. Munro and Chris Dearden
ISBN 978 1 84310 272 4

Safeguarding and Promoting the Well-being of Children, Families and Communities
Edited by Jane Scott and Harriet Ward
ISBN 978 1 84310 141 3

Understanding Costs and Outcomes in Child Welfare Services

A Comprehensive Costing Approach to Managing Your Resources

Lisa Holmes and Samantha McDermid

Jessica Kingsley *Publishers*
London and Philadelphia

Cover image supplied by www.shutterstock.com

First published in 2012
by Jessica Kingsley Publishers
116 Pentonville Road
London N1 9JB, UK
and
400 Market Street, Suite 400
Philadelphia, PA 19106, USA

www.jkp.com

Library of Congress Cataloging in Publication Data
Holmes, Lisa.
Understanding costs and outcomes in child welfare services : a comprehensive costing
approach to managing your resources / Lisa Holmes and Samantha McDermid.
p. cm. -- (Child welfare outcomes)
Includes bibliographical references and index.
ISBN 978-1-84905-214-6 (alk. paper)
1. Children--Services for--Great Britain. 2. Child welfare--Great
Britain-- Finance. I. McDermid, Samantha. II. Title.
HV751.A6H65 2012
362.7068'1--dc23
2011037315

British Library Cataloguing in Publication Data
A CIP catalogue record for this book is available from the British Library

ISBN 978 1 84905 214 6
eISBN 978 0 85700 448 2

Printed and bound in Great Britain

Contents

List of Tables

List of Figures

List of Boxes

Preface

Understanding Costs and Outcomes in Child Welfare Services: A Comprehensive Costing Approach to Managing Your Resources aims to contribute to the evidence base of understanding the costs and outcomes of interventions provided to vulnerable children and their families.

This book brings together a number of studies carried out by researchers over the past five years at the Centre for Child and Family Research, Loughborough University, England. The text builds on and extends a methodology that was first developed in 2000 by Harriet Ward, Lisa Holmes and Jean Soper to cost services for looked after children and to understand the relationship between needs, costs and outcomes when providing services to these children (Ward, Holmes and Soper 2008).

The findings from the research are brought together and set within the policy and practice context in England. As with the aforementioned 2008 publication it should be emphasised that this book is not about cutting costs or reducing services, but about ensuring that limited resources are optimally used to benefit vulnerable children and their families. A point that is particularly pertinent at a time of substantive funding cuts to the public sector and a renewed focus on children's social care following the publication of the Munro *Review of Child Protection* – a comprehensive investigation of children's social care (Munro 2010; Munro 2011a; Munro 2011b).

This is a complex book and it could not have been produced without the assistance of a great number of people. The research included in the text has been supported by grants from the Department for

Education (formerly Department for Children, Schools and Families), the Local Government Association and also Action for Children. We are grateful for their support and in particular for the support and advice offered from members of the various research advisory groups.

The book would never have been completed without the editorial assistance of both Harriet Lowe and Suzanne Dexter, whose support and attention to detail have been invaluable. To all the other members of the team who have been involved in the costs and outcomes programme of research, in particular to Harriet Ward and Jean Soper, without whom the programme of research would never have been developed. Thanks also to Joe Sempik, Clare Lushey, Doug Lawson, Matthew Padley, Paul Dyson and Mike Gatehouse who have all been involved in the data collection or analysis across one or more of the various studies.

Finally, we particularly wish to thank all the local authorities and service providers that have participated in the research, for taking the time to complete various surveys and for taking the time to speak to members of the research team. Most importantly we express our thanks to all the children and families that have contributed either by completing online surveys or agreeing to meet with one of the research team. We hope that the methodology and findings from the research will help to improve service provision in the future.

CHAPTER 1

Introduction

Introduction

At a time of public spending cuts and an increase in the demand for child welfare services in England it is essential to examine how and who can deliver services effectively and efficiently to vulnerable children and their families. But, how do we know if services have been effective? Or whether services have been provided efficiently, or at the right time? Have decisions to provide ongoing support and services been cost or needs led?

This book brings together findings from a number of studies carried out by the Centre for Child and Family Research (CCFR) at Loughborough University to explore the relationship between needs, costs and outcomes of services provided to vulnerable children. The book explores how information about costs, the needs of vulnerable children and the outcomes they achieve can be brought together to provide an evidence base for commissioning and planning services to children and their families. By understanding the unit costs of services and how they relate both to children's needs and outcomes it is possible to understand how limited resources can be used most effectively. Moreover, this book aims to place the child at the centre of understanding the relationship between needs, costs and outcomes by focusing on the pathways for individual children. It also outlines a methodological approach that aims to provide evidence to plan and commission the support and services required to ensure that all children have opportunities to flourish into adulthood.

Previous studies carried out by the Centre for Child and Family Research (CCFR) have shown that it can be particularly costly to provide services to looked after children (Ward, Holmes and Soper 2008), to children with complex educational, behavioural and health needs (Holmes, Westlake and Ward 2008) and to those with disabilities (Holmes, McDermid and Sempik 2010). Spiralling costs, concerns about public spending, together with evidence of unsatisfactory outcomes for vulnerable children and young people, have led to a need to introduce greater transparency and understanding of the relationship between needs, costs and outcomes of welfare services provided to all vulnerable children. High quality information about vulnerable children is required if children's services departments' commissioning strategies are to be effective, as was advocated by Care Matters (Department for Education and Skills 2007). Other government initiatives in England in recent years such as Quality Protects, Choice Protects, and Invest to Save have also increased the focus on accountability, assessment of outcomes and cost effective planning and commissioning of social care for vulnerable children. As a result of the growing squeeze on public spending, the onus has increased on service commissioners to ensure that they are procuring the most cost effective services; to achieve the best possible outcomes for vulnerable children and families from finite budgets (McDermid *et al.* 2011). Therefore, a comprehensive understanding of how finite resources, both financial and otherwise, are effectively distributed is essential to ensure that the right services are provided at the right time, to the children who need them most.

Background

In England local authorities have a statutory duty to provide services, or to facilitate the provision of those services, to all children identified as being in need living in their area. Section 17 of the Children Act 1989 states that a child or young person is in need if s/he is: 'unlikely to achieve or maintain, or have the opportunity of achieving or maintaining, a reasonable standard of health or development without the provision for him/her of services by a local authority', if his or her 'health or development is likely to be significantly impaired, or further impaired without the provision of such services' or if s/he 'is disabled' (Children Act, 1989).

Latest figures indicate that there are approximately 375,900 children in need in England (Department for Education 2010a), 64,400 of whom are looked after (Department for Education 2010b). The remaining 311,500 children in need will be receiving some level of support from children's services departments and other agencies, while remaining with their families. The priority to maintain familial care is built into the legislative framework of social care in England. The Children Act 1989, and subsequent social work practice, is founded on the principle that children are best cared for within their own families, and provision should be made to ensure that only those with the greatest needs should become looked after. This principle is underpinned in the Children Act (1989) by the notion parental responsibility and the local authority's duty to support children and their families and to return a child looked after by them to his or her family 'unless this is against his interest' (Department of Health 1989:1). While numerous children will be cared for by a local authority, many of those children will receive support within their own families prior to or subsequent to being looked after. The support services offered to such families represent a significant amount of the overall work undertaken by children's services departments.

Policy and practice context

In England over recent years there have been a number of developments in policy and practice, along with wider social factors such as the impact of the public's changing perception of child and family social work and the national economic picture that have influenced the context in which child welfare services are provided.

Refocusing in children's social care is not new (Axford and Little 2006): There has been a remarkable amount of change and reform in the children's social care arena since the 1970 Local Authorities Social Services Act (Munro 2010). Over the past 15 years, priority has been given to all children in need as a result of the impetus to refocus services following the publication of *Messages from Research* (Department of Health 1995). The New Labour government (from 1997-2010) set the policy context for the provision of services for all children in the white paper, *Every Child Matters* (Department for Education and Skills 2004). This document outlines the need for effective support and service provision for children in need and their families. Soon after taking office in May 2010, the Conservative–Liberal democratic coalition government commissioned a comprehensive, independent review of Child Protection in England (Munro 2010; Munro 2011a and 2011b). It was intended that the Munro review would examine the current condition of children's social care services, with a focus on strengthening the social work profession and to make policy and practice recommendations to facilitate well-informed judgements based on up-to-date evidence in the best interests of children (Munro 2010). Such refocusing in policy and practice has raised the profile of social care provision for children not looked after.

Furthermore, the pace and volume of change implemented in recent years, has led to an increasingly complex, and fluctuating landscape of provision to children in need. Most notably, change has occurred in the following areas: the integration of agencies and greater choice of services and providers for families, increasing emphasis on prevention and early intervention, and local authorities being encouraged to make considerable efficiency savings.

Integration and service provision

The Children Act 1989 asserts that services should be needs led, and local authorities are encouraged to respond to local need (Department of Health 2000). Recent policy moves have emphasised the need to reduce central prescription and interference and place greater trust in local leaders and skilled frontline professionals (Department for Education 2011a). Consequently, both the structure of social work teams and the services they provide vary considerably between local authorities (Ward *et al.* 2008; Holmes, Munro and Soper 2010). In addition, recent moves towards greater integration between partner agencies and multi-agency delivery of services have exacerbated this variability. *Working Together to Safeguard Children* (Department for Children, Schools and Families 2010) states that 'safeguarding and promoting the welfare of children - and in particular protecting them from significant harm - depends on the effective joint working between agencies and professionals' (p 3). Integrated working has previously been underpinned by Children's Trusts (Department for Children, Schools and Families 2010). These were local area partnerships led by the local authority, which bring together the key local agencies, some of which are under a statutory 'duty to co-operate', to improve children's wellbeing through integrated services focussed on delivering the five Every Child Matters outcomes. Children's Trusts have since been formally dispersed by the Coalition government. However, in some areas multi-agency partnerships have become embedded into practice and continue to operate at a local level bringing together public, private, community and voluntary sectors to work together to provide services to all children in need and their families.

Furthermore, in recent years, local authorities have played a greater role in the commissioning of services provided by the independent sector, rather than the provision of services directly (Ward *et al.* 2008; Gatehouse, Ward and Holmes 2008). The Coalition government has set out plans to support commissioning strategies, along with the introduction of initiatives such as payments by results (Cabinet Office 2011). It is envisaged that 'The Big Society' initiative is also likely to widen the spread of service providers, with voluntary and community groups playing an important role in the provision of services at a local level (Allen 2011a).

Such changes have resulted in considerable diversity in commissioning, procurement, funding and delivery arrangements across local authorities. Consequently, the types of services on offer to support vulnerable children and families may vary considerably across localities and any service provided as a result of a child being identified as in need may be funded or delivered by a range of providers, including statutory, voluntary and independent agencies (Ward *et al.* 2008; Holmes, McDermid and Sempik 2010).

Impact of preventative and protection policies

Over recent years the increased emphasis on prevention and early intervention has resulted in the parameters defining those children who may be considered to be 'in need' of additional support becoming increasingly ambiguous. The 2002 Spending Review recommended that prevention services become mainstreamed (France *et al.* 2010), and more recently the Allen Review advocated the increased focus on early intervention and prevention (Allen, 2011a). Subsequent policy moves towards preventative services (Department for Education and Skills 2004; Her Majesty's Treasury *et al.* 2005; Department for Children, Schools and Families 2007; Allen 2011a) have resulted in the introduction of a wealth of prevention and early intervention strategies and *additional services* at both national and local level (Axford and Little 2006; Statham and Smith 2010), supported by a range of evidence to suggest that such services are highly effective and efficient (Allen 2011a). These include the introduction of targeted services for 'vulnerable families' or universal services located in areas of identified higher need. Vulnerable children, defined more broadly than children in need, are those children who have 'acquired or encountered some difficulty that requires additional help if their life chances are to be optimised or the risk of social exclusion averted' (Preston-Shoot and Wigley 2005:257).

Services aimed at supporting vulnerable families include those offered by Sure Start children's centres and the introduction of the Common Assessment Framework (CAF) (Department for Children, Schools and Families 2007). A CAF is a shared assessment and planning framework for use across all services and agencies working with children and families. It has been designed for use with children and families with additional needs, but who do not meet the threshold for more intensive interventions such as those associated with safeguarding or social care. CAF aims to help the early identification of children and young people's additional needs and promote co-ordinated service provision across a range of agencies and professions to meet them (Children's Workforce Development Council 2009). The Children Act 2004 gives greater emphasis on orientating provision to ensure improved outcomes for all children, rather than those most in need (Axford and Little 2006). Consequently, prevention has become central to the work undertaken by all agencies working with children and families, including social care. As one study reported 'earlier intervention is a cornerstone of government policy on supporting children and families' (Statham and Smith 2010:10).

Research has highlighted the complexity of conceptualising and defining early intervention, identifying those who require it, and evaluating its impact and effectiveness (Statham and Smith 2010; Robertson *et al.* 2010; Holmes *et al.* 2010). Ward *et al.* (2008) suggest that this shift in focus, consolidated by the implementation of CAF, has resulted in a blurring of the boundaries between work that is undertaken specifically with children identified as being in need as defined by section 17 of the Children Act, and those receiving universal or targeted service provision as a result of being identified as having additional needs and therefore requiring additional support through a CAF assessment (Ward *et al.* 2008; Holmes, McDermid and Sempik 2010; Holmes, Munro and Soper 2010). While front line workers within social care have a functional understanding of thresholds between these two groups of children the boundaries are conceptually less clear for commissioners and mangers when considering the numbers of families accessing their services. Similarly, across a range of agencies there appears to be lack of understanding of boundaries and thresholds for the involvement of social care services (Holmes, Munro and Soper 2010; Holmes, McDermid and Padley forthcoming).The Common Assessment Framework is designed to be undertaken by any practitioner in any agency, which may not necessarily involve the support or provision of services from Children's Service's Departments. Consequently, children who may be receiving support services as a result of a CAF may not be known to social care, or their details recorded on any management information system. As such, there is a possibility of underestimating the numbers of families and children receiving support from social care and other agencies and the costs of supporting them (Gatehouse, Ward and Holmes 2008). At the time of writing there is not a universal and/or systematic system for recording CAFs or linking data to that of social care management information systems. It is therefore not possible at present to follow a child's pathway through CAF and social care services, despite evidence to suggest that CAF is being used in some local authorities to support children as they return home from being looked after, or once safeguarding processes are ceased

(Holmes, Soper and McDermid 2011). While a national electronic recording system for CAF, national eCAF, has been piloted by 20 local authorities (Department for Education 2011d) at the time of writing, there are no plans to roll this system nationally. Individual local authorities may need to explore local systems for linking data on those families receiving support and services as a result of a CAF with other data.

Social care in the public and political spotlight

Alongside preventative work, children's services departments have a duty to protect children assessed to be at risk of significant harm (HM Government 2006). However, it is evident that children's social care has come under substantial scrutiny from practitioners, policy makers and the public in recent years. A number of high profile cases which attracted substantial media attention, such as the tragic death of Peter Connelly (Department for Education 2010c; Department for Education 2010d), the subsequent 2009 report by Lord Laming; *'The Protection of Children in England'* (Laming 2009) and the Government's action plan (Cm 7589 2009) have brought child protection and the functionality of Children's Social Care into the political spotlight. Government and policy makers have emphasised the need to critically examine children's social care and ensure that social workers and the structures that support their work are fit for purpose. The comprehensive investigation carried out by the Munro review was commissioned for this purpose (Munro 2010; Munro 2011a; Munro 2011b). The Interim phase of this review highlighted a number of concerns, observing that well intentioned reforms have in fact had untendered consequences such as the bureaucratisation of social work, the emphasis on top down regulation and New Public Management to the detriment of empowering social workers to autonomous exercise judgement based on their training and rapport with individual families (Munro, 2010).

Munro's review, along with others, also notes that high profile cases, such as that of Peter Connelly, has impacted on the workloads and morale of current workers and difficulties in recruiting new staff (Social Work Task Force 2009; Holmes, Munro and Soper 2010).

Local authorities have seen greater levels of anxiety with regards to the safeguarding of children among social care practitioners and colleagues working in other agencies. (Holmes, Munro and Soper 2010). Front line workers and managers have reported that such an environment has increased the burden placed on social care referral and assessment teams. Under such conditions, frontline workers have also expressed concerns regarding their own morale and capacity to complete all the tasks necessary for high quality assessments (Baginsky *et al.* 2010; Holmes, Munro and Soper 2010). This is further compounded by difficulties in recruiting new social workers to the profession. The Social Work Task Force noted that 'social workers feel that their profession is under-valued, poorly understood and under continuous media attack. This is making it hard for them to do their jobs and attract people into the profession'(Social Work Task Force 2009).

Increased anxiety about safeguarding is reflected in the considerable rise in the number of referrals made to social care. A study published by the Association of Directors of Children's Services (ADCS) based on responses from 105 local authorities identified there had been a 24.6% increase in initial contacts between October–December 2007 and the same quarter in 2009 (Brookes 2010). In England, social care assessments are carried out across a range of levels: Initial Assessments at the referral stage; Core Assessments in cases where families are considered to have more complex needs (Millar and Corby 2006); and section 47 Enquiries are conducted in the case of safeguarding concerns. Practitioners participating in a number of studies have reported an increase in the complexity and needs of the cases allocated to them (Brooks 2010, Holmes, Munro and Soper 2010, Holmes *et al.* 2010). The ADCS study found that there had been an increase of 20.3% in the number of section 47 enquiries being undertaken, and a 32.9% increase in the number of children subject to a Child Protection Plan. While the numbers of children referred to social care has been steadily rising over recent decades, this rise has accelerated since the publicity around the death of Peter Connelly (Munro 2010). National statistics from the Department for Education show there was an 11% increase in the referral in the year following his death and a further 10.4% increase the following year (Department for Education 2010a).

The Department for Education report that around 65% of the referrals were progressed to an initial assessment in 2009-10 (*ibid*). Frontline practitioners working in referral and assessment teams reported that they had received an increased number of referrals that were not considered to meet the threshold for social care intervention, which they considered to be taking time away from effectively completing assessments for those that did meet the threshold (Holmes, Munro and Soper 2010), along with placing undue anxiety on vulnerable families (Munro 2011). These findings support those identified elsewhere, that further training may be required to support practitioners in other agencies with a clearer understanding and guidelines regarding the thresholds for social care intervention (Gilligan and Manby 2008; Ward *et al.* 2008; Norgate, Triall and Osborne 2009; Easton, Morris and Gee 2010). Despite the rise in demand for services, the study with 105 local authorities carried out by ADCS identified that staff levels had only risen by 10% (Brookes 2010). Concerns have been expressed by practitioners and managers that due to increased demand for services, and increasing pressure on social care teams, thresholds have been set so high that many families with considerable needs are not being given adequate support or access to necessary services (Holmes, Munro and Soper 2010; Sheppard 2008a; Sheppard 2008b).

Cost effectiveness and the economic context

Corby (2006) notes that when children's services departments operate under two agendas, that of providing good quality preventative services and of ensuring highly effective child protection services for those children at the greatest risk, the pressure to manage finite resources and the need for better models of cost calculations are both greatly increased. While prevention and protection should not be seen as competitors, more stringent fiscal control may be required within local authorities to ensure that resources are reoriented towards preventative services without child protection services suffering (Axford and Little 2006; Sheppard 2008a).

This book has been prepared as the United Kingdom has come out of the most severe and synchronised recession since the Great Depression. Concerns about public spending are at the forefront of current social policy in England. The new coalition government has announced plans to reduce the national debt through tightening the public finances by a total of £113bn by 2014-15, with £61bn of this coming from a reduction in government expenditure. The Government has highlighted that there is a need to cut public spending, not as an end in itself, but rather as an essential step on the path towards long-term, sustainable, and more balanced growth. Growth and fairness are the stated aims of the government in making decisions about spending cuts. The Government aims to achieve the elimination of unnecessary expenditure, while prioritising funds on the areas that matter most to the UK (Alexander 2010).

One such strategy is to invest in early intervention strategies to produce longer term savings (Allen 2011b). There is some evidence to suggest that along with promoting positive outcomes early intervention and prevention services, are highly cost effective, minimising the likelihood of needs and difficulties from escalating, and subsequently reducing the need for more intensive and costly services, such as intensive interventions or specialist residential care, for some children at a later stage (Beresford 1994; Chan and Sigafoos 2001; Farrington and Welsh 2004; Axford and Little 2006; Ward, Holmes and Soper 2010; Allen 2011a). Furthermore, Allen (2011a) notes that:

> 'People who have adverse early childhood experiences can end up costing society millions of pounds through their lifetimes, both in direct spending to cope with their problems and behaviours and in the indirect loss of output and tax revenues from themselves and those they affect' (p.24)

Statham and Smith (2010) state that while the arguments for the potential for early intervention to save money have been popular among policy makers and practitioners, attempts to demonstrate this through empirical research have proved challenging. Measuring the possibilities of savings involve a number of assumptions including the capability to identify those who would otherwise go on to develop poor outcomes and those who may receive a earlier intervention service who would otherwise achieve good outcomes if left unsupported (Statham and Smith 2010; see also Munro 2010). Better data are required if reliable costs and effectiveness evaluations of early intervention strategies are to be undertaken. It is evident that the ability to follow children and young people trajectories and the costs of the services they receive is essential in understanding the long term impact of a range of interventions and support.

While, at the time of writing, it is unclear the extent to which such public spending cuts will impact children's social care. It is evident, however, that local authorities will have to make difficult decisions in providing services to meet children's needs while satisfying government demands for spending cuts. There is some early evidence to suggest that local authorities have already experienced a cut in some frontline services due to reductions in public spending and that these cuts are likely to increase during the next financial year (2011-2012) (Holmes *et al.* 2010; Holmes, McDermid and Padley forthcoming).

It is evident that the landscape of children in need services is highly complex. This highlights the need for a robust costing methodology to clarify costs and help to ensure that services are most effectively deployed to achieve best possible outcomes for all children in need.

The costs and outcomes research programme

This book outlines an approach to calculate the costs of support and services provided to vulnerable children, highlights how these costs can be linked with children's needs and outcomes and also outlines the findings from a number of studies carried out as part of the costs and outcomes research programme at the Centre for Child and Family Research (CCFR), Loughborough University.

The programme of research, which started in 2000, aims to explore the relationship between needs, costs and outcomes of child welfare interventions. The first study in this programme explored the costs and outcomes of placing children in care (Ward, Holmes and Soper 2008) and developed a 'bottom up' costing methodology that has since been utilised across the programme. Subsequently the methodology has been implemented for the calculation of costs of child welfare services across a range of areas including education and health services for looked after children (Holmes and Jones forthcoming; Holmes *et al.* forthcoming); specialist therapeutic placements (Holmes, Westlake and Ward 2008); short break services for disabled children (Holmes, McDermid and Sempik 2010) and key policy and practice developments (Holmes, Munro and Soper 2010).

The costing method is a process driven approach that begins by separately costing the individual activities undertaken by professionals to support a child or family. Activities are broken down into their most discrete components, and linked to data concerning salaries, overheads and other types of expenditure, and allows one to build up a detailed and transparent picture of unit costs. Multiplying the unit cost of providing a service to a child by the frequency with which it is delivered gives the cost of providing the service to the child during the time period under consideration. Costs are calculated individually for each intervention that every child receives and are then aggregated in different ways to show the total cost for selected groups of children or for particular types of services during the relevant time period.

This approach of breaking down social care activity into its most discrete parts places the child at the centre of cost calculations. The initial study which focussed on looked after children (also referred to as children in care) identified that along with variations in local authority policies and procedures; and variations in service types, costs vary according to differences in children's needs and characteristics (Ward, Holmes and Soper 2008). The method clarifies the various ways in which children with different needs and circumstances are supported differently by social care and other agencies and therefore allows these differences in need and circumstances to be accounted for in cost calculations. Given the uniqueness of children's characteristics and the services they may receive the method introduces transparency into cost calculations, allowing the effectiveness and relative costs of different configurations of services provided to children with different types of needs to be examined. Costs, therefore reflect a child's perspective and experience of the support received over time (Beecham 2000).

As part of the ongoing research programme the team have developed a decision analysis model, a software tool (the Cost Calculator for Children's Services) to facilitate the calculations and to bring together the different types of data: unit costs of ongoing support and services; finance information and child level data, including data items relating to children's needs and circumstances (Ward, Holmes and Soper 2005; Soper 2007). The model has been developed to make use of routinely collected national data sets, for example the SSDA 903 data for looked after children and the Children in Need Census.

Making use of the Cost Calculator for Children's Services, the approach facilitates the exploration of costs over time, increasing the understanding of cost fluctuations and indicating how costs relate to reported outcomes. The ongoing research programme has demonstrated that there is only a relatively small disparity between the final figures produced by the 'top down' and 'bottom up' methodologies for calculating the costs of local authority care, and much of the differential may be explained by anomalies in the calculation of overheads (Selwyn *et al.* 2009). Furthermore, the method introduces transparency and consistency into cost calculations by clarifying what is included (Beecham 2000) and exposing factors influencing variations in costs (Holmes, McDermid and Sempik 2010). In addition, the research programme takes a systems approach to cost calculations, whereby the impact of changes in costs in one area of service provision on another can be explored. For instance, how changes in the cost of social care referral and assessment processes may impact on other agencies such as those implementing the Common Assessment Framework. Consequently, the method provides comprehensive information regarding the costs of meeting the needs of a diverse range of children and families, and can be used to ensure that finite resources are distributed according to the levels of need.

The studies

This book brings together the findings from a number of studies undertaken by the research team at CCFR over the past four years (2007-2011). These studies include a Department for Education (formerly Department for Children, Schools and Families) funded study to extend the methodology that was developed for looked after children for all children in need (Holmes *et al.* 2010). This study aimed to calculate the costs of support and services provided to a sample of children in need as defined by section 17 of the (1989) Children Act. The study also aimed to identify any factors that led to variations in costs. Preliminary work was carried out with 15 local authorities to map the range of services that they provided to children in need. In-depth research was then carried out with four local authorities.

This book also draws on two studies that focussed on the provision of short break services for disabled children: a Department for Education funded study to calculate the costs of short break services across a sample of local authorities and voluntary providers along with an evaluation of Action for Children short break services (Holmes, McDermid and Sempik 2010; Holmes *et al.* 2010; McDermid *et al.* 2011). The DfE funded research was carried out with three local authorities and two voluntary providers, the study explored both the costs of referral processes as well as the costs of providing different types of short break services. The evaluation of Action for Children short break services explored the impact of the services on outcomes for children and their families. The study was carried out across eight Action for Children services including residential and family based overnights, activity holidays and community based short break services.

The findings from a Local Government Association (LGA) funded study are also included. This research explored the cost and capacity implications for local authorities of implementing Lord Laming's (2009) recommendations. The potential financial and capacity implications were explored for a set of six key recommendations (numbers 11, 15, 16, 19, 20 and 24), with an emphasis on referral and assessment processes, case-loads, along with appropriate levels of supervision, training and support. A national survey was completed by 46 of the 152 local authorities in England and in-depth research was conducted in nine authorities.

This text also draws on findings from other recently completed studies, including the research to cost a specialist treatment programme for children and young people with emotional or behavioural difficulties. This research explored the costs of the Multidimensional Treatment Foster Care programme for adolescents and compared placement costs with other types of placement provision for children with similar needs (Holmes, Westlake and Ward 2008). The findings from two Knowledge Transfer Partnerships are also referred to throughout this text, one of the partnerships focussed on the costs of assessing and providing support and services for children with special educational needs and the second focussed on exploring the costs of health services and support provided to looked after children.

Finally, the emerging findings from a study recently commissioned by the Department for Education to explore the costs and impact of the Common Assessment Framework are introduced.

Book outline

The conceptual framework for the process driven approach to costing services is introduced and explained in Chapter 2. A focus is placed on the distinction between ongoing support provided by practitioners working with families, and other agencies to support vulnerable children and their families; referred to as '*case management activities*' and the provision of services.

The 'bottom up' methodology to calculate unit costs of the *case management activities* is outlined in Chapter 3. This includes a stepped approach detailing all of the data and information that is required to undertake a 'bottom up' costing exercise. Chapter 4 focuses on the services that are provided to vulnerable children and their families, both how the information is recorded at an individual child level and also how the services can be costed consistently to facilitate cost comparisons between services.

Variations in costs according to children's needs and linking these with outcomes form the basis of Chapter 5. This chapter brings together the different elements of the methodology outlined in the three previous chapters and highlights how the methodology can provide evidence to understand a child's journey.

Chapter 6 explores how aggregated costs can be used both to inform the research knowledge base but can also be used practically for both policy and practice development. The wider messages for policy and practice are framed within the context of longer term, life time cost implications within Chapter 7.

Throughout the book, illustrative case studies and 'cost timelines' are used to demonstrate how the methodology relates to the experiences and circumstances of individual children[1]. The case studies are based on data gathered as part of the studies outlined above. The names of the children and some of their details have been changed in order to preserve their anonymity. Worked examples based on the studies outlined above are also included to provide detailed breakdowns of how unit costs have been calculated and used.

The authors have endeavoured to write this book to present a research evidence base that can be used to inform policy and practice and as such have attempted to facilitate the use of the chapters as standalone texts. The methodology has also been presented in such a way to facilitate replication of the methodology by practitioners, managers, service providers and other interested parties. There are a number of complimentary resources that also facilitate the calculation of unit costs using a 'bottom up' approach, that can be utilised alongside this book (see Beecham 2000; Holmes, Lawson and Stone 2005; Curtis 2010; McDermid 2010; Curtis forthcoming).

Unit cost calculations

The unit costs included in this book have been calculated at different times, during different financial years across a range of studies. In order to facilitate comparisons where necessary, the unit costs have been inflated to 2010-11. Where costs have been inflated this has been done by using the Personal Social Services Research Unit (PSSRU) pay and prices inflators and the Treasury GDP deflator estimate (see Curtis 2010).

---

1   Throughout this text, for brevity the authors have used the term 'children' to refer to all children and young people.

Chapter 1: Summary

- Children's social care in England has been subject to substantial political and public scrutiny in recent years. In an attempt to scrutinise and systematise the structures in place to support vulnerable children and families, the focus on the child can be lost. This book aims to ensure that the child remains at the centre of understanding costs and how those costs can be linked with needs and outcomes.

- The policy and practice context of services provided to children in need is highly complex and varied. This is compounded by integration and early intervention strategies which have blurred the boundaries demarcating which children are defined as being in need under section 17 of the (1989) Children Act, and the services that are provided to them. The introduction of the Common Assessment Framework may also result in an underestimate of the number of children receiving support and services from social care and other agencies.

- Government policy has focussed on services provided to children in need, particularly in relation to the prevention of poor outcomes. In addition, greater focus has been placed on protecting children from harm and evidence suggests that referrals have increased to social care, placing increased pressure on the capacity of social work teams.

- Comprehensive and accurate information can aid the planning and commissioning of services, ensuring that finite resources can be most effectively deployed.

CHAPTER 2

The Conceptual Framework

Introduction

This chapter outlines the conceptual framework that has formed the basis of the process driven costing methodology (introduced in Chapter 1). The conceptual framework was first developed by the research team at CCFR to calculate the costs of placing children in care (Ward, Holmes and Soper 2008). The aim of the original study was to link the costs of services for looked after children more closely with the children concerned by taking all the cost drivers into account and identifying the factors that related to specific variations both in costs and outcomes (Ward, Holmes and Soper 2008). The ethos behind the conceptual framework was to develop a methodology to better understand the costs of providing services to looked after children, by understanding the social care support that was provided to them from the point of entry for the duration of their care episode. This approach was a move away from the 'top down' calculation of costs that focussed only on placement fees or allowances and calculated costs based on total expenditure. Therefore, this approach distinguishes between the monies paid for the placement in the form of fees and allowances from the costs of *case management activities* undertaken to support that placement. These activities to support looked after children were organised into eight processes.

The eight processes were initially modelled on the nine case management operations that underpin the task of looking after children in care or accommodation, outlined in the Core Information

Requirements (process Model, Version 2) Level Two Process 1.4 (Department of Health 2001a). It was necessary to make changes to the model to reflect practice, based on discussions, interviews and focus groups carried out with social care practitioners as part of the original study (Ward, Holmes and Soper, 2008).

The processes for looked after children, along with a brief description of each are outlined in Box 2.1. These processes are not linear, and not all looked after children will go through all the processes. Some children may experience some of the processes more than once within a given time period, for example a looked after child is likely to have two reviews (Process 6) within 12 months. Further details of how the processes are built up and used are detailed in Chapters 3, 5 and 6.

Identification and categorisation of activities

Each process is broken down into its constituent parts. Within each of the processes, all of the activities carried out by a range of social care professionals have been identified. The activities to be included in each of the processes were determined following exploration of local authority policy and procedure documents and then subsequent discussions with key personnel across local authorities.

The activities have been divided into two distinct categories: 'direct work' with children and their families, including both face-to-face meetings and telephone calls and also 'indirect work', including attendance at meetings of professionals and record keeping along with administrative tasks such as the completion and distribution of minutes. This method of breaking down the process into these two distinct categories was developed from the approach used in the Children in Need Census when it was first introduced in 2000, and in subsequent Census data collections until 2005. (Department of Health 2001b; see also Beecham 2000) and has subsequently been used across all the studies in the CCFR research programme to explore proportions of time spent on different types of tasks (Ward, Holmes and Soper 2008; Holmes, Westlake and Ward 2008; Holmes *et al.* 2009; Holmes, McDermid and Sempik 2010). Such an understanding of the different ways that social workers and other

Box 2.1: Eight social care processes for looked after children

Process 1: Decide child needs to be looked after and finding the initial placement

This process determines whether the child should be looked after; a decision based on an assessment of the child's needs. Once this decision has been made a placement will be identified and the appropriate procedures undertaken to place the child.

Process 2: Care planning

Assessment of the child's needs during the time they are looked after covers a number of developmental domains. The Care Plan form is updated following a review meeting (Process 6).

Process 3: Maintaining the placement

While the child is living away from home the social worker continues to maintain contact to support the child and facilitate links with the family. The cost of this process also includes providing the placement (placement fees or charges, allowances paid to carers, etc.).

Process 4: Child ceases to be looked after

This process occurs when the child leaves the care system. This may be because they return home, are adopted or make the transition to adulthood.

Process 5: Finding a subsequent placement

Some children might require a new placement. In either planned or emergency placement changes, this process of finding a new, appropriate placement that meets the child's needs is carried out.

Process 6: Review

An initial review meeting for looked after children in England should occur within the first 28 days of the child being placed. There is a second review within the first three months and subsequent reviews at six-monthly intervals. All the activity prior to and after the review meeting is included.

Process 7: Legal processes

For some looked after children legal orders must be obtained, such as a care order under section 31 of the Children Act 1989. This absorbs considerable social work time as well as that of the local authority Legal Department.

Process 8: Transition to leaving care services

In England some children will come under the provision of the Children (Leaving Care) Act 2000. Shortly before their 16th birthday responsibility for these care leavers is transferred to another team who undertake a detailed assessment of their needs (Pathway Plan).

social care professionals use their time is essential in evaluating both the efficacy and the costs effectiveness of a service and can provide valuable information for the workload management and resourcing of social care teams (Munro 2010). Box 2.2 outlines some examples of the types of activities included in the conceptual framework. Further details and exploration of the time spent on the different types of activities is explored in Chapter 3.

Box 2.2: Examples of activity types

- Direct contact with family
- Contact with professionals in relation to case
- Attendance at meetings in relation to case
- Writing of reports or case records
- Travel
- Other

Exploring variations in costs

Central to the aim of the original study was to develop a methodology that enabled variations in the costs of placing children in care to be identified and explained, introducing transparency into cost calculations. Ward, Holmes and Soper (2008) identified three key drivers for variations in costs: variations in local authority policy and procedures resulting in differences in the types of *case management activities* undertaken with children; variations in the types of placements provided, and variations in the needs and circumstances of the children. To differentiate cases where variations occur, a 'standard case' was identified as a child with no identified additional care needs, placed in local authority foster care within the local authority area. The difference between standard cases and those with variations is explored further in Chapter 3.

Extension of the conceptual framework
for all children in need

One of the key findings from the original research study was that shortages of resources and funding for looked after children had led to local authorities raising the thresholds for children being placed in care or accommodation. Consequently those children who became looked after were more likely to be amongst the most needy and difficult to engage (Ward, Holmes and Soper 2008). Furthermore, the study highlighted the need to understand more about the relationship between the needs, costs and outcomes of the children's pathways prior to them being placed in care or accommodation, in particular those children who were already known to children's social care and as such were in receipt of support or services as a child in need. As outlined in Chapter 1, there are currently in the region of 311,500 children in need supported in their families (Department for Education 2010a) who will be receiving various levels of support from social care and other agencies. In order to fully understand the costs of supporting vulnerable children and families, it is necessary to explore the costs of children in need who remain supported with their families.

To extend the framework to all children in need a preliminary mapping exercise was undertaken with 15 local authorities (Ward *et al.* 2008). The mapping exercise sought to ascertain which services were most commonly accessed by children in need and what data were available for those services, with the aim of identifying the set of services that could most usefully be included in cost calculations. A mapping template was constructed to identify all services each participating local authority either solely or jointly funded or commissioned to support those children identified as being in need as defined under section 17 of the Children Act 1989. The template was based on a framework developed in an earlier study (Soper *et al.* 2006) and was designed to tabulate comprehensive information on all services accessed by children in need. For each authority, the team initially populated the template with data gathered using publicly available documentation, such as Children and Young People's Plans, the online children's services directories and the local authorities' websites. The partially completed overall maps were then presented to the local authorities, with guidelines for completion by their key staff.

Completion of the mapping study template proved to be a useful but time consuming task for the participating authorities. The original study identified that the different cost components of providing support and services to looked after children were clearly distinguishable and could be categorised as 'the placement'; *case management activities* and wrap around services provided by other agencies to support the child in their placement, for example, youth offending or mental health services. However, the mapping exercise highlighted the variety and complexity of types and configurations of support and services provided to children in need. It was therefore harder to distinguish the elements into discrete components for costing. The sheer volume and complexity of children in need services resulted in the research team carrying out numerous additional interviews and informal discussions with different practitioners within the local authorities. This complexity was compounded where established partnership arrangements with other agencies were in place. Data were not always readily available to populate the framework, particularly where services were jointly commissioned or jointly provided. Access to financial data for individual services was problematic for some of the authorities.

However, using the information from the completed templates it was possible to identify a set of core *'additional services'* in each participating local authority. Core *additional services* were defined as those 'participatory services that were most frequently cited across the mapping authorities and that were reported to take up the highest proportion of the budget'. These criteria were used because they were likely to identify those areas in which there was the greatest investment of all resources (staff time and expenditure). Participating authorities were invited to comment on whether the proposed set of core services offered an accurate reflection of their authority, and some adjustments were made.

Categories of services

Mirroring the original study the mapping exercise identified two distinct types of services. Those in the first category provide 'ongoing support' or *case management activities*, whereby a social care professional manages and supports the day to day needs of a case. In addition to any direct contact with the child and family, this activity can constitute assessments undertaken with the child or family, regular planning and reviews, administration and liaising with other professionals in order to support the case. The work is carried out by allocated social workers and other practitioners in social work teams such as team managers, family support workers and team administrators.

The second category of services comprise *additional services* for children in need and their families, enabling them to attend groups, parenting classes, or sessions aimed at addressing specific needs. These *additional services* may be provided either by the same team as those performing 'ongoing support' activities or by another team, agency or provider. The categorisation, recording and provision of *additional services* is explored in Chapter 4.

To fully reflect the conceptual distinction between activity types and to extend the approach earlier 'process' driven approach the *case management activities* function was separated from the other *additional services* accessed by children in need and their families. Such a separation partly reflects a functional split to distinguish between activity related to maintaining and managing an ongoing case and any additional activity to support the child, as provided by the local authority or by an external agency. The distinction was a development and enhancement of the model utilised in the original study which also facilitated an exploration of the different data sources and recording of the two types of activities within children's services departments.

Processes providing ongoing support to all children in need

As with the original study the *case management activities* for children in need were based on the case management operations outlined in the Core Information Requirement Process Model (Department of Health

2001a). The case management operations in the Process model were mapped against proposed child in need processes. An additional process, 'ongoing support', was included to reflect the day to day support offered to families. The participating authorities were then consulted on the pilot set of child in need processes. The processes were organised in such as way as to best reflect social work practice as reported in discussions with practitioners. The eight processes for children in need are shown in Box 2.3 along with their definitions.

It was evident from the set of case management processes for looked after children outlined in Box 2.1 and those for children in need outlined in Box 2.3 that each set of processes can be organised under the broad areas of 'pre-assessment activities'; 'assessment and decision making'; 'provision of the service'; 'planning and review'; legal interventions' and 'close', as shown by Table 2.1.

TABLE 2.1: The relationship between the case management processes for looked after children and those for children in need

ACTIVITY AREA	CASE MANAGEMENT PROCESSES FOR LOOKED AFTER CHILDREN	CASE MANAGEMENT PROCESSES FOR CHILDREN IN NEED
Pre-assessment activity		Process 1: Initial contact and referral
Assessment and decision making	Process 1: Decide child needs to be looked after Process 5: Finding subsequent placement	Process 2: Initial Assessment Process 5: Core Assessment Process 7: section 47 Enquiry
Provision of service	Process 3: Maintaining the placement	Process 3: Ongoing Support
Planning and review	Process 2: Care Planning Process 6: Review Process 8: Transition to leaving care services	Process 6: Planning and Review
Legal interventions	Process 7: Legal processes	Process 8: Public Law Outline
Close	Process 4: Child ceased to be looked after	Process 4: Close child in need case

The processes outlined in Box 2.3 have been designed to operate in conjunction with the eight social care processes for looked after children. All of the processes except Process 3: Ongoing support, are

Box 2.3: Social care processes for all children in need (not looked after)

Process 1: Initial contact and referral

The process is concerned with the activity undertaken from the point at which a concern is raised about a child or a referral is made to children's social care.

Process 2: Initial assessment

This includes activity carried out to complete the initial brief assessment of a child's needs including the need for protection and the nature of services required. This methodology assumes that this activity begins once an initial referral to a caseworker has been made (Process 1).

Process 3: Ongoing support

This process constitutes all the ongoing activity to support the child for the duration of the case being 'open' and to achieve the outcomes outlined in the Child in Need or Child Protection Plan.

Process 4: Close child in need case

This process includes activity to close a child in need case when he/she no longer needs to receive support from social care. In many ways, this process is a continual process that happens alongside Process 3. However, the focus of this process is at the point that the child no longer requiring support as outlined in the Child in Need Plan.

Process 5: Core assessment

This process covers the in-depth assessment of a child's needs which addresses the central or most important aspects of the needs of a child and capacity of his or her parents or caregivers to respond appropriately to those needs.

Process 6: Planning and review

Child in need or child protection case conference reviews are carried out, where the child's development and welfare are discussed. This process includes any preparation and follow up work as well as the time spent at the actual review meeting.

Process 7: Section 47 enquiry

This process covers the in-depth assessment of a child's needs where there may be a child protection concern.

Process 8: Public Law Outline

This process captures activity when the courts, parent partnership services, legal advisors and other council legal or youth justices become involved in a case. Primarily this process will be concerned with activity to complete the Public Law Outline.

discrete events, which may happen over a period of days, but have clear start and end points. Process 3 differs conceptually in that it is a continued process throughout an episode of need. The unit cost of this process has been calculated per month (see Chapter 3 for further details).

All children in need will go through the first four of these processes during their time receiving support from social care. Families may be referred to social care by another professional, an agency or a member of the public. In some cases families will contact social care directly to access services. Once a referral has been made, and the case is determined to meet the threshold for intervention, an Initial Assessment will be undertaken to establish the needs of the family and to develop a plan of support which is subsequently delivered as part of the ongoing support until such time as the child is no longer deemed to be in need and the case can be closed.

If the case remains open, the child's plan will be reviewed at six monthly intervals and an updated plan will be developed. In some cases, further assessment may be required and a Core Assessment may be undertaken, or a section 47 Enquiry if there are concerns that the child may be at risk of significant harm. Additional assessments may take place at any time. In most cases a Core Assessment or section 47 Enquiry will be undertaken shortly after the initial contact and referral; in others they may take place after a review concludes that the present support is not sufficiently meeting the needs of the child and family. Jack's story below describes how these processes might be carried with a child.

Box 2.4 Jack's story: Part 1

Jack was aged 11 at the start of the study and lived with his mother and had no siblings. Jack was referred to social care in October 2008 by his teacher after concerns about his violent and disruptive behaviour. After discussion this with Jack's mum concerns had also been raised about their relationship, in particular the ability of his mum to deal with his tantrums and use appropriate levels of discipline.

An initial assessment was undertaken by a social worker from the referral and assessment team who felt that Jack was in need as defined by Section 17 of the Children Act, due to 'family dysfunction'.

Jack and his family were allocated a social worker from the Children in Need team who visited on a regular basis. His case was reviewed in March 2009 and Jack's care plan was updated to reflect the discussions at the review. Support continued until the end of the study.

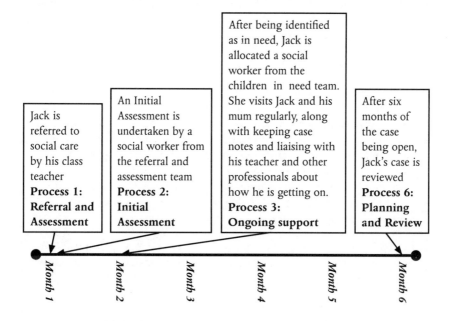

FIGURE 2.1 Timeline for Jack

Children on the edge of care

Extending the original conceptual framework to include all children in need, allows for the exploration of the inter-play between the looked after and children in need systems in England. In particular it becomes possible to follow a child's journey from referral to children's social care through to becoming a child in need or looked after, if appropriate. It also facilitates an analysis of how costs can build up over time and how decisions made in the shorter term can impact on longer term costs (Ward, Holmes and Soper 2008).

Furthermore, previous studies have identified that support episodes for children in need do not always operate in isolation, children may move in or out of care or accommodation or may be adopted (Holmes, Westlake and Ward 2008; Ward, Holmes and Soper 2008; Munro 2011a). Similarly looked after children may receive substantive support from social care under section 17 of the Children Act before becoming looked after and also following a care episode. The sequence of moving in and out of care may be

---

Box 2.5: Case study Ruby's story

Ruby was five and a half at the start of the study and had been receiving support from social care for 14 months prior to the data collection. Ruby was first referred to social care in August 2007 and had been receiving support as part of a Child Protection Plan. Her parents were identified as regular drug users and it was considered that this was impacting on their ability to care appropriately for her needs. In particular, her mother's chaotic lifestyle and regular drug use meant that she frequently failed to get Ruby up and ready for school. The home environment was felt to be unsuitable for young children.

Ruby lived with her mother, and had regular contact with her father who also misused drugs. Both parents were reluctant to engage with additional services.

In early December 2008, Ruby's social worker was contacted by a child care worker at a children's centre who reported that Ruby presented with bruises, allegedly caused by her mother's new partner. Along with concerns regarding the lack of improvements since the implementation of a Child Protection Plan, further investigation was instigated and the decision was taken for Ruby to be placed in local authority foster care. A review was held 28 days after she was placed and the Care Plan updated following that review.

---

repeated several times. The cost model needs to function consistently for such children so that the costs of them changing care status can be explored.

The example of Ruby shows how the two sets of processes, those developed for children in need, and those developed for looked after children relate to one another.

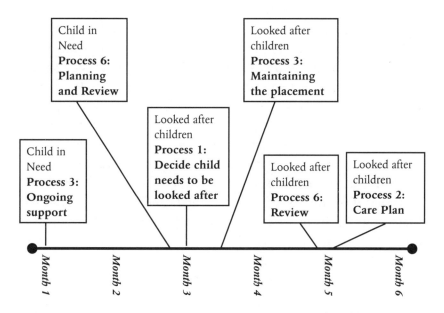

FIGURE 2.2 shows how the two sets of processes, for children in need and looked after children align to follow a child's journey through the two social care systems.

Disabled children accessing short breaks

As outlined in Chapter 1, section 17(c) of the Children Act (1989) defines all disabled children as children in need. Disabled children and their families will receive a range of services including short break services. In 2007 the Green Paper, Aiming High for Disabled Children: better support for families (Department for Children, Schools and Families 2008) outlined a range of measures to improve services for disabled children, including short break provision. The Green Paper also led to the introduction of a 'local core offer model' that aimed to reduce bureaucracy and improve access to short break services. Supported by The Children and Young Persons Act, 2008, Aiming High for Disabled Children (AHDC) places a duty on every local authority in England and Wales to provide services designed to assist individuals and families caring for disabled children. This duty was strengthened in 2011, when a statutory duty on local authorities to provide a range of short break services was introduced (Department for Education 2011b). Short breaks can be delivered in the form of overnight stays, day, evening and weekend activities and can take place in the child's own home, the home of an approved carer or a residential or community setting (Department for Children, Schools and Families 2008). The central aim of short break provision is to provide disabled children enjoyable experiences away from their primary carers, and parents and families a necessary and valuable break from their caring responsibilities.

However, accessing appropriate short break services for disabled children can be a difficult task for families (Robinson, Jackson and Townsley 2001; McConkey, Truesdale and Confliffe 2004; Carlin and Cramer 2007). In many cases specialist assessments are required to gain access to various services. Parents caring for disabled children in receipt of a number of services can suffer with 'assessment fatigue', with multiple, perceivably lengthy assessments being carried by a number of agencies or professionals (Holmes, McDermid and Sempik 2010).

In 2009, CCFR were commissioned to carry out a study to calculate the costs incurred by children's services departments of providing short break services to disabled children and their families. The study aimed to calculate the costs of individual services, provided by both local authority and voluntary service providers. In addition, and in order to calculate the full range of costs associated with the provision of short breaks, the study aimed to identify and calculate the costs of the routes by which families are able to access short break provision, and any ongoing social care activity undertaken to support the child and family once in receipt of short break services.

Two types of access routes were identified and costed for comparison: the 'traditional' assessment and referral route, which included an initial or core assessment, resource allocation panels, and assessments carried out as part of the Common Assessment Framework; and a 'local core offer model' whereby a local authority

Box 2.6: Case management processes for disabled children receiving short breaks

Referral and assessment

Process 1: Local core offer model

The provision of a standardised package of short break services to a specific population of disabled children and young people, who meet an identified set of eligibility criteria. The services may be accessed without an additional assessment.

Process 2: Common Assessment Framework for accessing short breaks

The Common Assessment Framework (CAF) is a standardised approach to conducting assessments of children's additional needs and is designed to be undertaken by any professional working with a family.

Process 3: Initial assessment

This process is concerned with activity around the initial brief assessment of a child's needs including the need for protection and the nature of services required. The methodology assumes that this activity begins once an initial referral to a caseworker has been made.

Process 4: Core assessment

This process covers the in-depth assessment of a child's needs which addresses the central or most important aspects of the needs of a child and capacity of his or her parents or caregivers to respond appropriately to those needs.

Process 5: Resource panel

These panels consist of senior and other managers, and are designed to enable discussion and decision making regarding individual cases. Social workers who identify a need to provide a service to a child may have to make a written case and may attend the meeting to present their case to senior managers before authorisation for a service can be given. Administrative support may also be provided to the panel.

Ongoing provision

Process 6: Ongoing visits

These are the regular visits undertaken to support disabled children and their families. You will need to include the travel time to and from visits, and any case recording undertaken after a visit in the overall time. You will also need to consider how frequently visits are undertaken for children with different kinds of needs.

Process 7: Reviews

This process covers the activity for the review meeting, where the child's development and welfare and the family's needs are discussed. This process is concerned with any preparation and follow up work undertaken as well as the time spent at the actual meeting.

offered the provision of a standardised package of short break services to a specific population of disabled children and young people, who meet an identified set of eligibility criteria. The case management processes for families receiving short breaks are outlined in Box 2.6 and related to either the referral and assessment or ongoing social care activity undertaken in order to support the family once the short break provision was in place.

Developing the model for other service areas

It has been possible to develop the conceptual framework, utilised in the original study, to other services areas. As noted in the introduction, the costs and outcome programme of research at CCFR has used the methodology to also explore services to children with special educational needs (Holmes *et al.* forthcoming) complex educational, behavioural and health needs (Holmes, Westlake and Ward 2008) and to those with disabilities (Holmes, McDermid and Sempik 2010).

Research carried out by CCFR suggests requests for services following an assessment are increasingly approved by a panel of senior managers (Holmes and Jones, forthcoming; Holmes, *et al.* 2010). These panels vary considerably across local authorities in their terms of reference, membership and use. Some local authorities require all requests for services to be approved by panel, while others only use panels for approving particular services or types of cases. The 'bottom up' methodology has been utilised to calculate the costs of these panels in a number of different service areas including short breaks (Holmes, McDermid and Sempik 2010), special educational needs (Holmes *et al.* forthcoming), services for vulnerable children and families (Holmes, McDermid and Padley forthcoming) and fostering (Holmes and Jones forthcoming). Emerging finding suggest that these panels can constitute a costly and relatively time-consuming process, and in some cases, can result in further delays before a service is received. However, there is evidence to suggest that regular panels will incur a lower cost than panels that are convened on an ad hoc basis (Holmes, Sempik and Soper 2009).

The definition of a child in need and the introduction of the Common Assessment Framework

The previous chapter explored how recent policy moves towards preventative intervention and a focus on 'vulnerable families' have resulted in disparities in how individual authorities define a child in need. Section 17 of the Children Act 1989 states that a child or young person is in need if s/he is: 'unlikely to achieve or maintain, or have the opportunity of achieving or maintaining, a reasonable standard of health or development without the provision for him/her of services by a local authority', if his or her 'health or development is likely to be significantly impaired, or further impaired without the provision … of such services' or if s/he 'is disabled'. Some local authorities appear to adhere strictly to this and only provide services to those children who have been formally assessed as being 'in need' under section 17, referring on or not supporting other contacts.

If a child in need is defined as receiving support under section 17 of the Act then generally there should have been an Initial Assessment, and in this case there should be a record held by children's social care. Thus, there should be a basis for knowing the numbers of children using a service and its potential cost.

However, evidence from the mapping exercise as part of the children in need study suggested that the Initial Assessment commitment is being modified by the increased use of the Common Assessment Framework (CAF). If a child is receiving a service from another agency, they may not be known to children's social care or their details recorded on the Management Information Systems. The increased focus on early intervention and preventive services means that many children, who may be 'in need' may be receiving less intensive, but nonetheless essential, support services, such as those provided by children's centres, without any form of assessment by children's social care, or without being known directly to social care. One consequence has been a lack of clarity as to when a service becomes a service as defined under section 17 of the Children Act 1989 and which services should be recorded by social care. Another consequence is that without adequate data on the numbers of children receiving support, costs may be substantially underestimated (Gatehouse, Ward and Holmes 2008; McDermid 2008).

For the purposes of the study, given the availability of child level data, a child in need was defined as one who has undergone an Initial Assessment and is receiving subsequent support by social care teams. This definition is in line with the CiN Census guidance (Department for Children, Schools and Families 2009). However, it was evident from the study that further work may be necessary to explore the support children are receiving under CAF arrangements to accurately cost services to all children in need as defined by the Children Act 1989. At the time of writing this book, CCFR are completing a study to explore the costs and impact of CAF. A draft set of processes have been developed in line with existing processes for children in need and looked after children.

It is evident that the conceptual framework developed to explore the costs and consequences of placing children in care (Ward, Holmes and Soper 2008) can be utilised in a number of different areas of service provision. Each set of processes that have been developed within the costs and outcomes programme of research have been developed in such a way as to work in a complementary manner, making it possible to examine how a child might move between the different areas of service provision, or receive support from a number of the different service areas. Table 2.2 below shows the links between the case management processes for other studies in the programme and those for looked after children and children in need. While the emphasis in this book is on the costs incurred by children's social care, Table 2.2 provides an illustration of how the framework can be extended to other agencies, with the inclusion of the set of processes that have been developed for children with special educational needs (Holmes *et al.* forthcoming).

Additional service areas could also be incorporated and developed using the methodology. The costs and outcomes programme of research continues to develop the methodology as more service areas, and costs across a range of agencies are incorporated into the research. Additional sets of processes could be brought together with costs associated with the provision of the service in order to increase the evidence base. The overall aim of the costs and outcomes

TABLE 2.2: Case management processes across the research programme

ACTIVITY AREA	CASE MANAGEMENT PROCESSES FOR LOOKED AFTER CHILDREN	CASE MANAGEMENT PROCESSES FOR CHILDREN IN NEED	DRAFT CASE MANAGEMENT PROCESSES FOR CHILDREN WHO HAVE RECEIVED A CAF[1]	CASE MANAGEMENT PROCESSES FOR SPECIAL EDUCATIONAL NEEDS[2] (SEN)	CASE MANAGEMENT PROCESSES FOR DISABLED CHILDREN RECEIVING SHORT BREAKS[3]
Pre-assessment activity		Initial contact and referral	Intention to complete a CAF		Local core offer model
Assessment and decision making	Decide child needs to be looked after Finding subsequent placement	Initial Assessment Core Assessment section 47 Enquiry	CAF assessment completed	Finding education provision Children's Support Panel Assessment for Special Educational Needs	Common Assessment Framework Initial Assessment Core Assessment Resource panel
Provision of service	Maintaining the placement	Ongoing Support	Provision of ongoing support	Ongoing education provision	Ongoing visits
Planning and review	Care Planning Review Transition to leaving care services	Planning and Review	Multi-agency meeting	SEN Annual Review	Review
Legal interventions	Legal processes	Public Law Outline		SEN Disputes and Tribunal	
Close	Child ceased to be looked after	Close child in need case	Close CAF	Leaving education provision	

[1]. These draft processes are outlined in Holmes, McDermid and Soper 2011

[2]. These processes are outlined in Holmes et al. forthcoming

[3]. These processes are outlined in Holmes, McDermid and Sempik 2010

programme of research is to understand the full costs to the public purse of supporting vulnerable children and families. The continued development and extension of the research programme to fulfil this aim is explored further in Chapter 7.

The process driven model facilitates the modification of core elements of processes as practice changes over time or as new policies and initiatives are introduced. Adaptations have been made to two of the original case management processes for looked after children (Process 2: Care planning and Process 8: Transition to leaving care), to reflect changes in practice, including changes in the proportion of activity by different frontline practitioners. The process driven model enables ongoing adaptations. For instance, the Munro *Review of Child Protection* (Munro 2011b) highlighted the need to reduce 'top down' and centralised control and to support adaptability of processes and practices to meet local needs. The report recommends revising the Initial and Core assessments into one single assessment. This is being piloted in four local authorities at the time of writing (Department for Education 2011a). Therefore, were there to be future changes to the initial and core assessment processes, not only could the method outlined in this book facilitate the calculation of unit costs for the revised process(s) but also the consistent approach would allow an analysis of practice and process change.

This chapter has explored the conceptual framework on which the costs methodology is based; it has identified the three core cost components of *case management activities, additional services* and needs. How the various activities within the case management processes are bought together with financial data to calculate unit costs will be explored in the following chapter, and the remaining components will be explored in Chapters 4 and 5.

Chapter 2: Summary

- This chapter outlines the development of a conceptual framework for social care that identified two different types of activity carried out to support vulnerable children: *case management activities* whereby a social care professional manages and supports the day to day needs of a case and *additional services* such as groups, parenting classes, or sessions aimed at addressing specific needs. These *additional services* may be provided either by the same team as those performing 'ongoing support' activities or by another team or agency.

- The *case management activities* can be arranged into a set of processes for each of the service areas and can be organised around a set of categories.

- Each process is broken down into its component parts and includes activities such as direct contact with the child and family, contact with other professionals; attendance at meetings in relation to the case; case recording, other administrative tasks, and travel.

- The conceptual framework can be extended across a range of service areas, for both social care and other agencies to provide a consistent approach.

- The approach facilitates the exploration of variations in costs of providing both ongoing case management and *additional services*.

- The process driven approach facilitates the modification of core *case management activities* over time to reflect changes in policy and practice.

CHAPTER 3

The Calculation of Unit Costs

Introduction

The previous chapter outlined the conceptual framework on which the 'bottom up' unit costing method is based and that the methodology distinguishes between two different types of activities: *case management activities* which are organised into sets of processes, and *additional services.* The unit costs of these activities form the basic building blocks of the 'bottom up' costing methodology. The unit costs of different types of activities are bought together in order to calculate the costs of supporting an individual child or family, or group of children and families, over a given time period. This chapter outlines how the unit costs of *case management activities* are calculated, describes and analyses the different data collection methods that have been used and the resultant issues when the data are triangulated.

The principle of 'bottom up' cost calculations

The approach begins with the child, or group of children, and identifies the activities and resources which have been employed to provide different types of services, interventions or support, and uses these to build up costs from the 'bottom up'. The method is a process driven approach which begins by separately costing the individual *case management activities* (detailed in the previous chapter) undertaken by professionals to support a child or family. As outlined in Chapter 2, these activities are broken down into their component parts and organised into sets of processes (as outlined in Boxes 2.1,

2.3, 2.6 and Table 2.2). The time taken to complete these activities is linked to data concerning salaries, overheads and other types of expenditure to calculate a unit cost. Multiplying the unit cost of the *case management activities* and the costs of any *additional services* provided to a child by the frequency with which they were delivered gives the cost of providing support to the child during the time period under consideration. Costs are calculated individually for each intervention that every child receives and are then aggregated in different ways to show the total cost for selected groups of children or for particular types of services during the relevant time period. This approach allows one to build up a detailed and transparent picture of the costs incurred when providing support and services to vulnerable children and families.

Why calculate costs using the 'bottom up' method?

This approach of breaking down social care activity into its most discrete parts places the child at the centre of cost calculations. Previous research to explore the costs and consequences of placing children in local authority care (Ward, Holmes and Soper 2008; Holmes, Westlake and Ward 2008) used the same methodology to demonstrate how the costs of care reflect a complex relationship between the needs of children and the services they receive. For instance, Ward, Holmes and Soper (2008) identified that the children in the study sample with the greatest levels of need were frequently placed in the most costly placements, such as specialist residential placements or secure units. Furthermore, the study found that the time taken to complete *case management activities* varied according to the varying needs and/ or circumstances of the children. For example, the time taken, and therefore the cost, of finding and securing a placement for children who were defined as being 'difficult to place' (for example, children and young people with emotional or behavioural difficulties or those that had experienced prior placement instability) was higher than for other children in the sample.

Routinely published national data about the unit costs of children's services are usually calculated using a 'top down' approach (Department for Education 2010e). This method brings together relevant expenditure data and divides it by the number of children for whom the service is provided. Such calculations give an overall average cost per child but do not distinguish between variations in the needs and characteristics of the population served, the types of services necessary in supporting those users, or local circumstances or policies (Beecham 2000; Ward, Holmes and Soper 2008).

A 'bottom up' method allows more detailed cost comparisons because it can accommodate cost variations. By separately itemising the individual activities involved in delivering services to children in need and their families, 'bottom up' costing methodologies enable one to build up a detailed longitudinal picture of costs. It is possible to consider how children with different characteristics and needs require different types of *case management activities*, different *additional services* and follow different service trajectories and therefore incur different costs. The method clarifies the various ways in which children with different needs and circumstances are supported differently by social care and other agencies and therefore allows these differences in need and circumstances to be accounted for in cost calculations. Given the uniqueness of children's characteristics and the services they may receive the method introduces transparency into cost calculations, allowing the effectiveness and relative costs of different configurations of services provided to children with different types of needs to be examined. Costs therefore reflect a child's perspective and experience of the support received over time (Beecham 2000).

The method also facilitates the exploration of costs over time, increasing the understanding of cost fluctuations and indicating how costs relate to reported outcomes. Children and families, their needs, circumstances and capacity for resilience are unique, and are likely to change over time, requiring different care pathways and configurations of services.

The ongoing research programme at CCFR and work by other researchers has demonstrated that there is only a relatively small disparity between the final figures produced by the 'top down' and 'bottom up' methodologies for calculating the costs of local authority care, and much of the differential may be explained by anomalies in the calculation of overheads (Selwyn *et al.* 2009). The 'bottom up' method introduces transparency and consistency into cost calculations by clarifying and aligning what elements are included in all cost calculations (Beecham 2000) and exposing factors influencing variations in costs (Holmes, McDermid and Sempik 2010). Since the unit costs of the different *case management activities* and trajectories are calculated in a consistent manner, valid cost comparisons can be made for child, local authority and service variations.

The research programme has also adopted a systems approach to cost calculations, whereby the impact of changes in costs in one area of service provision on another can be explored. For instance, how changes in the cost of social care referral and assessment processes may impact on other aspects of the social care services provided by the Children's Services Department, or on other agencies such as those implementing and using the Common Assessment Framework. Consequently the method provides comprehensive information about the costs of meeting the needs of a diverse range of children and families, and can be used to assist decision making and planning to ensure that finite resources are distributed according to the levels of need.

The gathering of social care 'time use activity data' also makes it possible to examine issues around workload management and the division of social care personnel time on 'direct and indirect' activities. As noted in Chapter 2, activities undertaken by social care professionals can be distinguished as either 'direct activities' such as home visits and telephone calls, and 'indirect activities', such as attendance at meetings of professionals and record keeping along with administrative tasks such as the completion and distribution of minutes. Some reports have suggested that social workers spend up to 80% of their time on administrative activities (Herbert 2004; Munro 2011b). Critics have argued that attempts to improve social work practice through the introduction of targets and performance indicators has led to a focus on monitoring and auditing cases, requiring front line workers to record substantial amounts of data for both National Returns and to ensure their own professional accountability (Munro 2011a; Munro 2010; Burton and Van der Broek 2008). Concerns about the administrative burden placed on front line workers have been compounded since the introduction of electronic recording systems (Bell *et al.* 2007; Seneviratna 2007;

Broadhurst *et al.* 2009; Shaw *et al.* 2009; Holmes, McDermid, Jones and Ward 2009). It has been reported that electronic exemplars are too complex, time consuming to complete, and fail to reflect practice (Holmes *et al.* 2009). Furthermore, limited access to computers or remote access to management information systems has presented difficulties for social workers in being able to complete necessary paperwork and thus finalise assessments (Holmes *et al.* 2009). It has been possible to use the data to explore issues relating to the administrative burden placed on social care staff. This is discussed later in this chapter.

Collection of social care 'time use activity data'

'Time use activity data' has been collected to identify the average time spent by the various post holders to complete each of the social care processes outlined in Chapter 2. The data collection also sought to establish any variations in the times taken according to children's needs and circumstances, local authority variations or service type(s). The aim of the data collection is not to account for all social care practitioner time, rather gathering social care activity data allows for average times to be identified for specific types of cases.

It was evident from discussions with front line workers and managers across various studies undertaken by CCFR that workloads have been substantially affected by rises in initial contacts and referrals as outlined in Chapter 1. Holmes, Munro and Soper (2010) identified that concerns around social care teams' capacity to meet rising demand for services were prevalent. Workers reported having to make difficult decisions about how to prioritise cases, and in some instances, having to prioritise their work with children with the highest levels of need, over those who may benefit significantly from preventative work (see also Holmes, McDermid and Soper 2011). Furthermore, the recent scrutiny of social care and current policy reforms is driving a high rate of change within children's social care. It was apparent that authorities are experiencing the impact of these changes through restructuring processes and uncertainties about current and future funding levels (Holmes, McDermid, and Soper 2011; Ward *et al.* 2008 Action for Children 2011; Wood, Cheetham and Gregory 2011).

Data sources

The data collection methods to gather the 'time use activity data' were designed in such a way to reduce any potential additional burden being placed on local authorities participating in the research, in particular being mindful of the higher levels of workload that front line practitioners were experiencing. In many cases, the data collection methods were designed or adapted in consultation and collaboration with the participating local authorities.

To date three different methods have been used to collect data from local authority personnel: focus group discussions, verification questionnaires/online surveys and event records recorded on a daily basis for specific cases. These three different approaches were adopted to facilitate triangulation of the data by comparing the figures obtained from each method and also to utilise both retrospective and prospective methods of data collection. Each of these methods are outlined below.

Focus groups

The focus group methodology was used as a way of collecting information from as many workers as possible with the minimum of imposition. Focus groups are designed to encourage discussion among participants through some form of collective activity (Dobson 2004). The intention is to stimulate discussions among participants in order to produce a range of responses, thoughts and perceptions. Participants are encouraged to comment and discuss the views held by others in the group. The focus group facilitator encourages participants to discuss topics, challenge options expressed by others and present alternative experiences. Focus groups are particularly useful when exploring topics which the participants may not have reflected on before because they are encouraged to 'theorise, elaborate and possibly think about a topic for the first time' and therefore refine their own views on the topic at hand (Dobson 2004:285). By way of such discussions shared positions can be identified, ideas can be developed and refined in order to reach a consensus view (Henn, Weinstein and Forde 2006).

The purpose of focus group discussions carried out across the costs and outcomes research programme was to gain a broad consensus between practitioners on the time requirements of each of the case management processes that underpinned the delivery of the service. However, focus groups also enable a range of views, opinions and experiences to be expressed and are therefore an effective way of identifying variations in the time taken to complete case management process and also provide contextual practice information to frame the 'time use activity data'.

The discussion encouraged in the focus groups enables practitioners to identify and discuss variations in the time taken to complete *case management activities*, to discuss examples of cases where the case management processes may differ, and reasons for those differences, as well as reach a consensus about what might constitute an average case and an average amount of time (input) for that case. Focus groups therefore, produce rich data in a relatively short amount of time, whereby average process times can be identified, along with a great deal of contextual information about variations. The data gathered at the focus groups helped to build up a picture of front line social care practice. Issues such as changes in thresholds, caseload management and professional development were identified through the focus group discussions. Costs could, therefore, be calculated in a way that most accurately reflected social care practice.

Focus groups with front line practitioners and managers have been used extensively across the CCFR costs and outcomes research programme and have formed the basis of the social care activity data collection for the majority of the studies examined in this book. Where possible, the focus groups were convened as part of weekly team meetings, in order to facilitate access with as many workers as possible without the need to take up additional staff time. Practitioners responsible for *case management activities* were brought together and asked to estimate how much time they typically spent on each activity for each of the processes. Holding the focus groups by team brought together the various practitioner types and allowed the discussions to be centred on the processes that formed the core work of the particular team. The participants could work through these processes systematically and, since some processes involve more than one practitioner, each practitioner type could contribute estimated times for their element of input for each process. For instance, *Children in Need Process 2: Initial Assessment* is undertaken primarily by a social worker, with support from their team manager who initially allocates the case and checks and signs off the completed assessment. In some authorities administrative support is also provided to complete the process.

One of the key criticisms of focus group methods is the possibility or likelihood of bias being introduced by the presence of the researcher or other focus group participants (Dobson, 2004). Participants may be concerned about disclosing how long they spend undertaking certain tasks in front of colleagues, or the researcher. In order to reduce concerns it was emphasised at the start of focus groups that they have not been designed to establish whether individual workers' time is being used efficiently, rather that they are intended to elicit a range of responses. Workers were encouraged to report times based on their own practice regardless of whether they reported different figures to their colleagues and to utilise the focus groups as a forum to explore the reasons for these variations. Therefore, throughout the focus groups participants were encouraged to base estimates on their own experience, rather than on policy and procedure designations, or those of their colleagues. The time use activity estimates therefore relate to the reported amounts of activity undertaken by staff rather than to those stated in local or national guidance.

The focus groups have also provided an opportunity to discuss issues in relation to quality of practice and quality of assessments (Holmes, Munro and Soper 2010; Holmes, McDermid and Padley forthcoming). It has been possible to ascertain workers perceptions of the tasks that are required to carry out quality social care work with children and their families and the issues, such as increased workloads that impact on workers capacity and the need to prioritise certain tasks.

To summarise, by bringing together practitioners responsible for undertaking *case management activities* the purpose of the focus group discussions was to gain a broad consensus of the time requirements for case management processes that underpin service delivery and to identify variations. Where appropriate, the reported times spent on each activity for each professional involved were added together to produce a total figure, organised by job and activity type, for each process. Preliminary focus groups have also been used to pilot draft social care processes, for example the children in need and short break processes. Subsequently, focus group findings were also used to inform the design of verification questionnaires, the online surveys and event records.

Verification questionnaires / online surveys

The 'time use activity data' from the focus groups have been compiled into verification questionnaires which were used both to check the activity figures agreed through the focus groups and to collect any additional time use data that was either not conclusive, or was not covered in the focus group discussions. The questionnaires also enable additional data to be gathered from a wider cohort of participants. The questionnaires were structured around the social care processes, and respondents were required to identify how much time, on average, they spent on each activity associated with each process. A Likert scale was used, based on the range of times discussed in the focus groups, to avoid leading questions. Respondents were also asked to identify any variations in the time spent on each process. The questionnaires were broken down by process and practitioners were only invited to complete the questions relating to those processes relevant to their core work. The questionnaires were distributed to focus group attendees, and to their colleagues who were unable to attend the focus group meetings.

The verification questionnaires have subsequently been developed into online surveys for more recent studies to gather 'time use activity data' from large numbers of practitioners to increase the volume of data used for the calculation of unit costs. This approach has been found to be effective in engaging with a wider range of practitioners from a range of agencies and with a minimum of imposition (Holmes, Munro and Soper 2010; Holmes, McDermid and Padley forthcoming)

The original study which focussed on looked after children, based unit cost calculations on the findings from focus group discussions and follow up verification questionnaires (Ward, Holmes and

Soper 2008; Ward, Holmes and Soper 2005). Despite being open to criticism, the focus group consensus approach has been shown to have internal validity (Ward, Holmes and Soper 2008) and has proved to be robust across a range of studies undertaken by CCFR, in that there was little variation between reported times between teams and across participating authorities in relation to the amount of time spent completing standard tasks.

Event records

Since the completion of the original study the research team have introduced event records as a prospective method of collecting 'time use activity data'. Event records used in the studies examined in this book were based on the work of Byford and Fiander (2007). Event records generate specific data on activity times and complement the views of practitioners attending focus groups: they form a prospective tool that balances the retrospective 'estimates and opinions' (*ibid*; 20). This method of recording activity can place an additional burden on participants, so the event records themselves were designed in a way that made them simple and quick to complete. Participants were given the option of completing event records in either paper booklet or electronic format. Practitioners were only ever requested to complete an event record for *one* case on their current case load. For each activity undertaken for a sample case, workers were invited to record the type of activity, the process for which that activity was being undertaken, and the time taken to complete the activity. Workers were encouraged to complete the event record for a three month time period, an optimum length in order to capture ongoing support elements as well as discrete events (Byford and Fiander 2007; Holmes, Westlake and Ward 2008). A visit was held with each participating team prior to the data collection period to discuss the purpose of the event record data collection, to demonstrate how the event records should be completed, and to answer any questions or concerns. Practitioners were able to contact the research team to discuss queries and were encouraged to include free-text comments where appropriate.

Social care activity data collection: Methodological advantages and triangulation of data

The data collection methods outlined above were triangulated whereby data is gathered from multiple sources in order to increase the reliability and validity of the research (Becker and Bryman 2004). Organising the *case management activities* into social care processes enables the data to be gathered from a range of sources, while maintaining consistency of approach and internal validity. The three different data collection methods described above each use the social care processes to structure the data collection and analysis. This enables the data to be triangulated effectively. Data from a number of studies using the same methodology can be bought together to increase sample sizes and therefore the reliability and validity of the data. For example, social care 'time use activity data' relating to children in need has been gathered across two related studies: the research to explore the cost and capacity implications for local authorities implementing Laming's (2009) recommendations (Holmes, Munro and Soper 2010); and the extension of the cost calculator methodology for all children in need (Holmes *et al.* 2010). Combining the data in this way has facilitated the calculation of the unit costs based on data from a total of 11 focus groups across 11 local authorities and the inclusion of verification questionnaires/ online surveys from 71 frontline workers and managers, in addition to 35 event records.

Similarly the research team have been able to improve and update unit cost calculations for looked after children by increasing the amount of 'time use activity data' upon which the cost calculations are based. Data collection in the original study included 17 focus groups carried out across six local authorities, subsequent studies have provided additional data from 47 focus groups across a further six local authorities.

While the triangulation of the three different data collection sources has increased the sample size, bringing together the data has raised a number of issues for consideration. As with all self reporting methods the event records rely on workers accurately and consistently recording activities undertaken for a sample case (Becker and Bryman 2004). However, the conceptual differences in the processes present unique challenges for the data collection. With the exception of Process 3: Ongoing support, all the case management processes are discrete activities that have a clear beginning and end. For these discrete processes much of the activity data collected by event records were incomplete. This occurred because the timeframe for the completion of a process did not always fit into the study timeframe. Workers were asked to record information on whether additional activities had been undertaken for the processes before or after the event record time period, however, very few workers completed this section of the event record. Therefore, for all but Process 3, it is unclear whether the time recorded constitutes the whole process, and if not, how much of the process has been recorded. Furthermore, nearly two thirds (65%) of the event record entries were categorised by workers as being for Process 3. Thus, to date it has only been possible to utilise the event record data for the calculation of the unit cost of Process 3: Ongoing support. Work is ongoing to modify the event records and to explore adaptations that will increase their use for discrete processes in the future.

The focus group and questionnaire/online survey data yielded similar overall means for most of the processes. There were, however, notable differences in the range of reported values collected by the two methods in particular for Process 3 (ongoing support), with the questionnaire/online survey data producing higher reported times. This may be due to the retrospective nature of the design whereby the more complex cases are more memorable and the recorded times were based on those cases. In contrast, when complex cases were discussed at the focus groups they were differentiated as such, and the discussion continued until a consensus view was formed about how long activities usually take, thus reducing the possibility of bias from unusual or isolated cases.

The lower reported times for Process 3: Ongoing support in the focus group data may be attributable to difficulties identified in the conceptualisation of processes. The research has highlighted the difficulties in gathering retrospective data for ongoing *case management activities* (Holmes *et al.* 2010; Holmes, Westlake and Ward 2008). In the extensive work carrying out focus groups with social care professionals, it was evident that participants have difficulty in conceptualising the time spent on activities relating to ongoing support (Holmes, McDermid and Sempik 2010; Holmes, Westlake and Ward 2008), using the retrospective methods. The methodology requires activities to be broken down *per month, or per week per child* which is particularly problematic. By contrast, prospective methods provide a more reliable estimate of the ongoing activities carried out for Process 3. Such methods allow all activities to be included, from substantive activities such as home visits, to short activities such as leaving messages for other professionals. The smaller, less time consuming activities are easily missed in retrospective methods as individually they may only take a few minutes, but such activities can add up to more substantive quantities of time over a prolonged period. Focus group participants reported that discrete processes were easier to conceptualise. Therefore the methodological evidence to date suggests that the retrospective methods, of focus groups and verification questionnaires/online surveys are the most reliable for discrete processes, whereas, the retrospective method of using event records provides more accurate 'time use activity data' for the ongoing activities associated with Process 3.

Validating time use activity data: Scenario

Given the difficulties and complexities associated with the various data collection methods outlined above, it is important to measure the reliability and validity of the 'time use activity data' gathered, and the overall process times that are compiled, before they are used as the basis for unit cost calculations. The research team have utilised additional information gathered from practitioners to validate the 'time use activity data'. This validation procedure is carried out at various stages throughout the data collection period and allows for additional verification of the data as the collection of 'time use activity data' continues. The procedure facilitates calculations to explore whether it would be possible for the social care practitioners to undertake all the specified *case management activities* in an average working week, based on an average caseload and the overall process times. Scenario 1 in Box 3.1 provides an example of how the 'time use activity data' has been validated for the children in need processes.

Box 3.1: Validating standard process times

A full time social worker is usually contracted to work 37 ½ hours per week. Using the Personal Social Services Research Unit Cost schema (Curtis 2010) a social worker works 42 weeks a year, to allow for training, annual leave, sickness and statutory leave days. This amounts to 131 ¼ hours per month.

The average case load (for children in need cases), based on focus group data is 14 cases per full time social worker. The overall activity time for Process 3: Ongoing support was calculated to be 5 ½ hours for a social worker. Therefore, it can be estimated that on average a social worker spends 77 hours per month on ongoing support.

It is also possible to include the activity for planning and review. Children in need cases should be reviewed every six months. It can therefore be estimated that at an average case load of 14 this amounts to approximately 2.3 reviews per month. The average reported time spent on a child in need review is 7 hours and 40 mins. It is possible to estimate that social workers spend 17 hours and 40 minutes on reviewing activity per month.

Additional regular activities can also be taken into consideration. Based on data from the focus groups on questionnaires/online surveys, social workers reported that on average they spent 1 hour per month in supervision and 8 hours per month attending team meetings (based on a weekly meeting of two hours).

Each of these activities can be added together to estimate the time spent on regular activities per month.

ACTIVITY	MONTHLY ACTIVITY TIME
Process 3: Ongoing Support	77 hours
Process 6: Planning and Review	17 hours and 40 minutes
Supervision	1 hour
Team meetings	8 hours
Total	103 hours and 40 minutes

This leaves a full time social worker with 27 ½ hours per month to carry out irregular monthly activities such as undertaking assessments, the Public Law Outline, closing cases, and undertaking other activities.

The following scenario and all the unit costs that are calculated throughout this book are based on a 37 ½ hour working week (Curtis 2010). Frontline practitioners have consistently reported across all the studies within the research programme that it is not possible to complete their work within their contracted hours and that on average they worked in the region of 45 to 46 hours per week. This total did not include the additional hours they often worked completing paperwork and reading at home. All of the participating authorities operated a system of 'time off in lieu' (TOIL), where workers were entitled to take any additional hours, worked over their contracted time, off as leave. However, workers in each of the authorities anecdotally reported that they rarely were able to take all of their TOIL. In some cases this was because they regularly worked more than the allocated ten or 12 hours per month they were entitled to reclaim. A number of the workers stated that the pressures of work made it difficult to find 'time in the diary' to take TOIL (Holmes *et al.* 2009; Holmes, Munro and Soper 2010). However, basing the unit costs on the actual number of hours worked artificially inflates the unit costs once they are aggregated, and also introduces difficulties when the information is being used to explore workable case loads. There is also evidence to suggest that it is untenable for frontline practitioners to work these increased hours over the longer term (Holmes, Munro and Soper 2010), and therefore the unit costs need to be based on a long term achievable estimate of working hours.

The scenario above assumes that workload is evenly distributed and may not necessarily take into consideration fluctuations in workload. Focus group participants noted that external factors, such as school holidays, may increase their workloads at certain points in time. The scenario outlined in Box 3.1 does not take into account variations in time use activity according to the needs and circumstances of the children or differences in local policies and procedures. These variations and their impact on activity are explored in Chapter 5. The scenario does, however, demonstrate that the average process times are feasible and could be completed within an average working month and can therefore form the basis of unit cost calculations.

The unit costs of case management processes

Once the activity times have been identified for the social care processes, it is possible to calculate a unit cost for each process. The social care activity data needs to be linked to salary and overheads information in order to calculate the unit cost of each process. To ensure that the unit costs are nationally applicable, where available the national average salary scales for social care personnel have been used in the unit cost calculations (Wiggins and Storry 2010).The mean salaries for London and out of London authorities have been calculated. The London multiplier included in the PSSRU Schema outlined in the annual compendium of health and social care unit costs has been used to calculate a London cost (Curtis 2010). National average salary information was not available for social care administrators; therefore the average salary across the participating authorities for these administrative roles has been used. An hourly rate for each practitioner type was calculated, including on costs (such as national insurance) and overheads.

The calculation of overheads

The 'bottom up' approach applies overheads to salary information, expressed as a percentage of direct salary costs, to ensure that a comprehensive cost of service delivery is included. 'Overheads' costs are those that are associated with the overall functioning of a business or organisation working within its usual range. In many (but not all) cases, these are costs that do not change with the number of interventions provided. Examples include premises, management, Information Technology (IT), Human Resources (HR) and office running costs. Selwyn *et al.* (2009) have noted that some variations in the costs of different services may be a result of differences in the way that overhead calculations have been undertaken. Most notably differences in the costs of local authority services and those provided by independent providers may be attributable to the inclusion of different items in overhead calculations. Consequently, a full exploration of overheads using a standardised approach allows for transparency to be introduced into overhead calculations which enables more accurate cost comparisons between service providers.

Within the area of social care costs one widely-used estimate of the overhead costs is 15% of the salary of social care workers, plus a one off figure for capital overheads. This is the approach that has been used in the PSSRU series, Unit Costs of Health and Social Care (Curtis 2010). This value is based on the work of Knapp, Bryson and Lewis (1984), which includes costs associated with clerical support and management by the team leader. However, recent work suggests that this figure underestimates the full range of overhead costs (Selwyn *et al.* 2009). Costs for specific local authority services are often seen as those that are managed within a particular budget area or cost centre and include the direct costs of service provision (staff, materials and so on) but the costs of premises, higher management and other generalised services, such as human resources and ICT support, are often omitted simply because they are not paid for by that centre or a nominal, fixed charge is levied or accounted for.

In light of these issues Selwyn *et al.* (2009) developed a framework for the calculation of overheads (see Table 3.1), which has since been piloted (Holmes, McDermid and Sempik 2010) and subsequently been utilised in the other studies examined in this book. The framework classifies costs according to five main expenditure categories: Employee, Client-related direct payment, Agency function, Establishment and Other, each of which (apart from Other) is divided into sub-categories. This framework enables estimates of overheads to be calculated that are as precise and accurate as possible and is designed to introduce transparency into overhead calculations.

TABLE 3.1: Framework for expenditure allocation: Overheads

CODE 1	EMPLOYEE			
Code main	Main category	Sub category	Sub-allocation	Comment
1	Employee	1	Payroll including NI and SA	All payroll costs including National Insurance and superannuation of staff in the section or team; (includes temporary and sessional staff and support staff)
				List of staff roles and salary costs
				Identify staff involved in management, support and administrative roles (i.e. those not directly involved in service delivery).
				Estimate the time spent on other activities (e.g. training) of staff who deliver services. Such activities do not include case meetings which are directly connected with service delivery but do include strategic meetings, general team meetings, etc.
1	Employee	2	Other employee Costs Costs associated with staff carrying out their work	Transport and subsistence (how much of this is incurred as a result of travel in connection with cases?)
				training and staff development
				mobile telephones
				personal insurance
				membership of organisations and professional bodies
				medical, dental and other fees
Code 2	Client-related			
2	Client-related Direct payment	1	Allowances	Any allowances or grants paid regularly to clients (total amounts and description). Including travel.
2	Client-related Direct payment	2	Start up grants and other payments	Any one off payments (total amounts and description)

Code 3	Agency Function			
3	Agency function	1	Professional	Any professional fees and registration charges
Code 4	Establishment			
4	Establishment	1	Premises: All costs associated with premises and accommodation	Includes rent; heating; lighting; maintenance; security; cleaning Who (cost centre, department, etc.) is responsible for these costs? How are premises costs apportioned to teams or departments? Is a nominal charge applied? Are costs shared with other sections or departments? If costs/buildings are shared, between how many people?
4	Establishment	2	Running Costs General office costs	stationery, telephone (not mobiles), printing, newsletters, Company cars, leasing arrangements and servicing costs (how are charges levied, e.g. is a nominal charge made or are individual costs met?)
4	Establishment	3	Central Services	Costs paid for corporate services such as HR, IT and payroll administration Is a nominal or standard charge levied? or… How are central services costed? What is the total cost of services? For how many individuals/teams are the services provided? Organisational chart of department/section.
4	Establishment	4	HQ management Costs of senior management not included in budget	What is the overall management structure? Are nominal charges for management services levied? Organisational chart of department/section.
Code 5	Other			
5	Other	1	Any other items paid out but not listed above	All other costs, small team budgets

Use of the framework by the research team has identified overhead figures that are substantially higher than the 15% used previously for social care unit cost calculations. In the study to explore the costs of short break provision carried out across three local authorities (Holmes, McDermid and Sempik 2010), an average percentage of 36.6% was calculated. In the study to cost services to children in need (Holmes *et al.* 2010), full expenditure data were obtained from two local authorities. These authorities provided details of itemised expenditure for the children in need teams. Unfortunately, incomplete information was provided by both authorities for the costs of premises. Therefore an estimated value of 9.3% of payroll was substituted for the missing data, again based on the approach of Selwyn *et al.* (2009) and represents the best available estimate for the cost of premises used by social care personnel in local authorities. The calculated value of the overheads was 47.1% in one of the authorities and 42.4% for the other. Thus giving an average of 44.7%. This compares with a mean value for overheads of 43% of employee costs used by Selwyn *et al.* (2009).

Calculation of unit costs per hour

Using the salary and overheads information outlined above hourly rates have been calculated for each social care personnel type. As previously outlined in this chapter these are based on 37½ contracted hours and 42 weeks worked per annum, to allow for 20 days annual leave and ten statutory leave days. Ten days sickness leave and ten days for training have been assumed, as outlined in Curtis (2010). The annual salaries and costs per hour for the different social care personnel are shown in Table 3.2. Costs have been calculated separately for London and out of London authorities, in line with the approach that was adopted for the calculation of unit costs for looked after children in the original study (Ward, Holmes and Soper 2008).

TABLE 3.2: Social care average salaries and unit costs per hour[1]

SOCIAL WORKER		SOCIAL CARE PERSONNEL			
			TEAM MANAGER	ADMINISTRATOR	FAMILY SUPPORT WORKER
Out of London	Salary per annum (£)	£31,751.83	£42,845.82	£20,927.11	£22,878.90
		£28.71	£38.74	£18.93	£20.69
	Unit cost per hour (£)				
London	Salary per annum (£)	£36,832.12	£49,701.15	£29,832.47	£26,539.53
		£34.40	£46.42	£27.86	£24.78
	Unit cost per hour (£)				

[1] Salaries inflated to financial year 2010-11

Having outlined the methodology to calculate the unit costs for children's social care, the following section of this chapter outlines two detailed breakdowns of the calculation of unit costs for children in need processes and those processes undertaken to provide disabled children with short break services. The breakdowns build up all the elements, including the collection of 'time use activity data', the calculation of unit costs for each type of practitioner and then the aggregation of the units of costs for each of the processes outlined in Chapter 2.

Unit costs of processes for children in need

This section of the chapter outlines the data collection and calculation of unit costs from the study to extend the original methodology for all children in need (Holmes *et al.* 2010) and the work to explore the cost and capacity implications for local authorities implementing Laming's (2009) recommendations (Holmes, Munro and Soper 2010). The data collection methods described above were used to identify the social care activity time for the eight social care processes for children in need (see Chapter 2 for details of the children in need processes). In total, 11 focus groups were carried out across four participating authorities with a total of 79 participants. These participants comprised a range of practitioners including 14 team managers, 58 social workers, two family support workers and five administrators. Table 3.3 shows the breakdown of focus group participants.

TABLE 3.3: Focus group participants

TEAM	PRACTITIONER TYPE				TOTAL
	TEAM MANAGER	SOCIAL WORKER	FAMILY SUPPORT WORKER	ADMINISTRATOR	
Number of focus group participants	14	58	2	5	79

In total 71 verification questionnaires and online surveys were completed and 35 event records were completed. Purposive sampling was used to ensure that event record data was gathered for children with a range of needs. Selection criteria were specified by the research team, based on the findings from the focus groups and verification questionnaires/online surveys. Each of the participating teams was invited to select cases based on these criteria. A range of different needs types were identified for use in the event records. Table 3.4 shows the number of completed event records broken down by type of needs.

TABLE 3.4: Number of event records by type of needs

CHILD NEEDS TYPE	TOTAL
No additional needs	9
Child on child protection plan	5
Child with disabilities	7
Emotional behavioural difficulties	7
Child on child protection plan + Emotional behavioural difficulties	3
Child with disabilities + Emotional behavioural difficulties	3
Child with disabilities + Child on child protection plan + Emotional behavioural difficulties	1
Total	35

Participants were invited to complete the event records for a three month period, but this target was only met by six of the 35 workers (17%). The average completion length was just over two months, with the range being from three days to five months. Event records where there was less than 14 days of recorded activity were excluded from the analysis to prevent the data being skewed (n=2).

Taking into account the various methodological issues outlined above, for all the processes except Process 3, a median of the mean focus group and mean questionnaire/online survey reported values for each activity within each process was calculated. For Process 3: Ongoing support, the event record data were sufficiently robust to be utilised and, given the difficulties with the retrospective approaches for this specific process, the event record data alone were used to calculate unit costs for Process 3.

The median times for each activity were then totalled to calculate a total time for each of the professionals involved in each process, as the following example of the initial assessment (Process 2) shows.

TABLE 3.5: Social care activity time by professional type for Process 2: Initial Assessment

ACTIVITY	ACTIVITY TIMES IN MINS[1]		
	SOCIAL WORKER (N = 53)	TEAM MANAGER (N = 2)	ADMIN (N = 2)
Preliminary discussion with team manager	20 mins	20 mins	
Initial visit to family	75 mins		
Travel time to family (round trip)	60 mins		
Update case file info on management information system	40 mins		30 mins
Fact finding	65 mins		
Write up Initial Assessment paperwork	210 mins		
Feedback to referrer	25 mins		
Sign off/agreed by manager		30 mins	
Total Time	495 mins (8 ¼ hrs)	50 mins	30 mins

[1.] The times in this table have been rounded to the nearest five minutes. The cost calculations reported in Chapters 5 and 6 have been calculated using the actual average reported times

The activities outlined in Table 3.5 have been combined, by post holder, for each of the eight children in need social care support processes. These collated average times are outlined in Table 3.6.

TABLE 3.6: Standard social care activity time for the eight case management processes for children in need

PROCESS	STANDARD SOCIAL CARE ACTIVITY TIME BY PROFESSIONAL[1]		
	SOCIAL WORKER	TEAM MANAGER	ADMINISTRATOR
Process 1 - Initial contact and referral	5 hours and 55 minutes	30 minutes	10 minutes
Process 2 - Initial Assessment	8 hours and 15 minutes	50 minutes	30 minutes
Process 3 - Ongoing support (per month)	5 hours and 30 minutes	50 minutes	
Process 4 - Close case	3 hours and 40 minutes	2 hours	1 hour
Process 5 - Core Assessment	17 hours and 55 minutes	2 hours	30 minutes [2]
Process 6 - Planning and Review: CiN	7 hours and 40 minutes		30 minutes
Process 7 - section 47 Enquiry	15 hours and 45 minutes	1 hour and 40 minutes	30 minutes [2]
Process 8 - Public Law Outline	35 hours and 20 minutes	32 hours and 50 minutes	1 hour [3]

[1.] The times in this table have been rounded to the nearest five minutes. The cost calculations reported in Chapters 5 and 6 have been calculated using the actual average reported time.

[2.] In the absence of available data regarding the amount of time administrators spent on these processes, the reported time for Process 2: Initial Assessment has been used.

[3.] In the absence of available data regarding the amount of time administrators spent on this process, the reported time for Process 7: Legal process for looked after children (Ward, Holmes and Soper 2008) has been used.

Calculation of unit costs for the social care processes for children in need

For each of the eight CiN processes the hourly rates have been multiplied by the reported time spent by practitioners to calculate the unit cost of each process. Table 3.7 shows the out of London and London costs for each of the processes. The unit cost for Process 3: Ongoing support is shown per month.

TABLE 3.7: Unit costs of social care processes for children in need including overheads[1]

		UNIT COSTS PER WORKER (£)			TOTAL COSTS TO SOCIAL CARE (£)
		SOCIAL WORKER	TEAM MANAGER	ADMIN	
Process 1	Initial contact and referral				
	Out of London	169.14	19.37	3.15	191.66
	London	202.68	23.21	4.64	230.53
Process 2	Initial Assessment				
	Out of London	237.81	31.62	9.46	278.89
	London	284.96	37.89	13.93	336.78
Process 3	Ongoing support (per month)				
	Out of London	158.03	34.67	-	192.70
	London	189.37	41.54	-	230.91
Process 4	Close case				
	Out of London	1.93	77.47	18.93	98.33
	London	125.70	92.84	27.86	246.40
Process 5	Core Assessment				
	Out of London	513.01	79.58	9.46	602.05
	London	614.73	95.35	13.93	724.01
Process 6	Planning and review: Child in Need Review				
	Out of London	218.89	-	9.46	228.36
	London	262.30	-	13.93	276.23
	Planning and review: Child protection case conference review				
	Out of London	313.03	-	75.68	388.71
	London	375.09	-	111.45	486.54
Process 7	section 47 Enquiry				
	Out of London	451.91	64.38	9.46	525.76
	London	541.52	77.15	13.93	632.60
Process 8	Public Law Outline				
	Out of London	1,014.75	1,271.25	18.93	2,304.92
	London	1,215.96	1,523.32	27.87	2,767.15

[1]. Salaries inflated for financial year 2010-11

Variations in activity data and unit costs of children in need cases

The unit costs displayed in Table 3.7 provide standard costings, but do not account for any variations. As outlined in Chapter 1 the original research study to explore the costs of looked after children demonstrated that costs vary according to the needs of children, the type of placement and local authority policies and procedures (Ward, Holmes and Soper 2008). Subsequent studies have identified similar categorisations of variations in the costs of case management processes. These variations can be applied to cost calculations for an individual child, or groups of children, providing a more accurate representation of the costs incurred for providing different types of services, to children with different types of needs, in different circumstances and local authorities.

A number of variations in the amount of time required to complete various case management activities have been identified for children in need. Focus group participants noted that where an initial contact and referral results in the decision to take no further action, an additional 45 minutes activity is undertaken to feedback to the referrers and where appropriate, to put in place any community-based services. As previously noted, front line workers reported that they had received an increased number of referrals that were not considered to meet the threshold for social care intervention, and that dealing with these cases took time away from effectively completing assessments for those that did meet the thresholds (Holmes, Munro and Soper 2010). Given the additional activity time required to deal with the cases, it could be speculated that inappropriate referrals are exacerbating the pressures on an already stretched resource. Where children do not meet the threshold for social care intervention a Common Assessment Framework (CAF) should be encouraged, Holmes, Munro and Soper argue that:

> 'It may be beneficial for authorities to consider whether they could make efficiency savings [by] promoting more effective use of the CAF to reduce the time [social] workers are spending on ['front door' services, contacts and referrals] thereby freeing up more time to respond to 'appropriate' referrals and undertaking necessary assessments.' (2010: 48)

These findings support those of other studies, that further training may be required to support practitioners in other agencies to undertake assessments such as CAF, along with clearer understanding and guidelines about the thresholds for social care intervention (Gilligan and Manby 2008; Ward *et al.* 2008; Norgate, Triall and Osborne 2009; Easton, Morris and Gee 2010).

The unit cost of an initial contact and referral (Process 1) which results in no further action has been calculated at £213.19 for out of London and £256.33 in London.

Front line workers reported that when Process 2: Initial Assessment was carried out for a child previously known to Social Care (i.e. a previous referral), an additional 2¼ hours of activity was required to read the case history and locate back files (when appropriate). The unit cost of this variation has been calculated at £343.50 for out of London and £414.17 in London.

The research identified two process costs for Process 6: Planning and review: one for children in need, receiving support under section 17 of the Children Act; and one for the Case Conference Review held for children subject to a Child Protection Plan. The two costs reflect the different time reported for these two different types of case. Participating social workers reported that reviews held for children in need took just over 7½ hours and a Case Conference Review, was reported to take just over 10 hours. These times include any preparation prior to the meeting and any work carried out after, as well as for the meeting itself. This difference in time spent, is primarily attributable to the preparation of paperwork, which was reported to take just over 3¼ hours for the case conference, and 1 hour 10 minutes for the Children in Need Review.

Additional variations were identified for Process 7: section 47 Enquiry. Workers reported that in some cases additional activities may be undertaken, increasing the cost of this process. The section 47 Enquiry includes a strategy discussion, which workers reported, usually takes place by telephone and takes an average of 15 minutes. However, in some cases, where there appears to be a high level of concern about a child's wellbeing, or where a large number of professionals are involved, a meeting will be held. Questionnaire and online survey respondents reported that a strategy meeting was held in approximately 25% of cases and that this meeting constituted 5½ hours of activity, including contact with the professionals involved, making practical arrangements for the meeting, the duration of the meeting and writing up the minutes. The costs of a section 47 Enquiry where a strategy meeting is held, has been calculated as being £680.90 out of London and £818.58 in London (an additional £155.14 and £185.98 respectively, per strategy meeting). Furthermore, workers identified that additional activity is undertaken if an Achieving Best Evidence interview is required. This was reported to take an additional 6 ¾ hours of social worker time and just under 5 hours of team manager time. The total cost of a section 47 Enquiry which includes an Achieving Best Evidence interview is £915.65 out of London and £1,099.72 in London. Table 3.8 summarises the variations in costs calculated for a section 47 Enquiry.

Earlier studies in the costs and outcomes programme have shown that variations in costs correlate to variations in children's needs (Holmes, Westlake and Ward 2008; Ward, Holmes and Soper 2008; Holmes, McDermid and Sempik 2010). These studies all demonstrate that those children with the highest levels of need often require the most costly services. In addition, these children often require the most intensive and time consuming support from social care practitioners. Subsequently, the cost of social care processes for children with high levels of need are increased. Measuring and categorising the needs of children is a complex process and is explored further in Chapter 5.

TABLE 3.8: Unit costs of section 47 enquiries[1]

SOCIAL WORKER		UNIT COSTS PER WORKER (£)			TOTAL COSTS TO SOCIAL CARE (£)
		TEAM MANAGER	ADMINISTRATOR[2]		
Standard section 47 Enquiry	Out of London	451.91	64.38	9.47	**525.76**
	London	541.52	77.15	13.93	**632.61**
Section 47 Enquiry including strategy meeting	Out of London	607.07	64.38	9.47	**680.91**
	London	727.44	77.15	13.93	**818.52**
Section 47 Enquiry including Achieving best evidence interview	Out of London	649.73	256.46	9.47	**915.65**
	London	778.57	307.31	13.93	**1,099.80**

1. Salaries inflated for financial year 2010-11

2. In the absence of available data about the amount of time administrators spent on this process, based on previous research, the reported time for Process 2: Initial Assessment has been considered to be comparable and therefore is included in this process

The unit costs of social care processes for short breaks

As noted in Chapter 2, the same method for calculating unit costs has also been used to calculate the costs of short break provision for disabled children (Holmes, McDermid and Sempik 2010). The aim of this study was to calculate the costs incurred by children's services departments of providing short breaks to disabled children and their families. In addition to calculating the costs of different types of short break services, the study aimed to identify and calculate the costs of the routes by which families are able to access short break provision, and any ongoing social care activity undertaken to support the child and family once in receipt of any short break services. A set of processes was identified as part of this study, for children and families in receipt of short break provision, in consultation with the three participating authorities. These processes outlined in Chapter 2 and summarised in Box 3.2 below relate to either the route by which families accessed the short break provision or ongoing social care activity undertaken to support the family once the short break provision was in place.

Box 3.2: Social care processes for short break provision

Access routes:
Local core offer model
Common Assessment Framework
Initial Assessment
Core Assessment
Resource allocation panel

Ongoing Support:
Regular visiting
Service reviews

Two key types of access routes were identified: the 'traditional' assessment and referral route, which included an initial or core assessment, resource allocation panels, assessments carried out as part of the Common Assessment Framework and any other assessments undertaken as part of the referral route; and a 'local core offer model' whereby a local authority offers the provision of a standardised package of short break services to a specific population of disabled children and young people, who meet an identified set of eligibility criteria.

The costs of these processes were then calculated using the same methodology described above. Focus groups were conducted across the three participating authorities. In total 37 professionals participated in the focus groups. Questionnaires were distributed to the authorities where panel procedures were in place for decision making to allocate short break services. Completed questionnaires were returned by seven senior managers, four team managers and two administrators. Table 3.9 outlines the costs of the case management processes for short breaks.

TABLE 3.9: The unit costs of social care processes for short breaks[1]

	LONDON (£)	OUT OF LONDON (£)
Referral and Assessment		
Local core offer model	26.38	
Common Assessment framework	-	191.27
Initial Assessment	315.89	344.75
Core Assessment	729.83	518.80
Resource allocation panel	114.32	98.20
Ongoing Support		
Visits	102.08	78.74
Reviews	267.87	198.34

[1.] Salaries inflated for financial year 2010-11

All the participating authorities had 'local core offer models' in place. These are intended to enable all children identified as having a severe learning difficulty or physical disability to have access to a range of services, with minimum assessment. Two of the participating authorities required no further assessments to be undertaken by social care professionals for children meeting the criteria for the local core offer. In both cases, the majority of activity to refer children and their families into 'local core offer' provision was undertaken by lead professionals from other agencies who are likely to have already undertaken some form of assessment. Therefore, costs to social care per child are estimated to be nominal. One local authority required all requests for short break provision to be agreed by a multi-agency resource panel. At the time of the study, only one local authority was routinely using the Common Assessment Framework to enable access to short breaks.

Additional exploration and analysis of the data

This chapter has explored all the data elements required to calculate unit costs of children's social care, using a 'bottom up' methodology. Another advantage of this approach is that by breaking down the *case management activities* into their component parts it is possible to carry out additional exploration and analysis of the data. The following section of this chapter outlines how the time use data can be explored to consider 'how practitioners spend their time', with a particular focus on proportions of time spent on direct work with families and on office based activities. The involvement of different practitioners, how their roles overlap and the impact of increased workloads are also discussed.

How social workers spend their time: Direct and indirect activities

As noted in Chapter 1, concerns have been raised that an increasing administrative burden has been placed on social workers, deflecting them from working directly with children and families, and that they spend a substantial proportion of their time carrying out administrative activities (Herbert 2004; Munro 2011b; Holmes *et al.* 2009; Munro 2004; Garrett 1999; 2003; Audit Commission 2002). Amid such concerns it has been possible to analyse the 'time use activity data' collected across a range of studies to explore the proportion of time spent on direct and indirect activities to support both looked after children and children in need. This analysis provides valuable information about workload management and resourcing social work teams (Munro 2010).

As part of the original study to explore the costs of placing children in care the research team ran a series of focus groups with social work practitioners in six local authorities in England and

Wales between 2001 and 2002 to gather activity data on the amount of time they typically spent on the eight case management processes for looked after children (see Ward, Holmes and Soper 2008). Between 2007 and 2008, the research team ran a further series of focus groups with social work practitioners to gather data on the same activities in six other local authorities as part of the ongoing programme of research explored in this book. Both sets of focus groups also explored key issues that affected social work practice in the participating authorities. In response to concerns about the increased administrative burden placed on social work practitioners these two sets of 'time use activity data' were brought together to explore changes between the two time periods (Holmes *et al.* 2009).

This exploration identified that both the average case loads of social workers working in teams to support looked after children and the total number of hours worked had risen between 2001 and 2008 (see also Holmes, Munro and Soper 2010). This may reflect the rise in demand for services discussed in Chapter 1 (Munro 2011b; Brookes 2010). Furthermore, the *time* spent on administrative both activities and indirect work for most of the social care processes had increased between the two time periods. Table 3.10 shows the time spend on different types of activity for each of the eight social care activities in the two data collection periods (It was not possible to distinguish between direct and indirect activities for Processes 4 (Return home), 5 (Find subsequent placement) and 8 (Transition to leaving care services) in the first data collection period).

This does not, however, reflect an increase in the *proportion* of hours spent on indirect activities for most processes, as the subsequent data collection also identified additional direct activities with children and their families. Table 3.11 shows the *proportion* of overall time spent on direct and indirect tasks across the eight social care processes for looked after children.

TABLE 3.10: Reported time spent on different types of activity for each of the eight social care processes for looked after children[1]

PROCESS	REPORTED TIME SPENT PER PROCESS[1]							
	DIRECT CLIENT RELATED ACTIVITY		INDIRECT CLIENT RELATED ACTIVITY		TOTAL	
	DATA COLLECTION 1 2001/2001	DATA COLLECTION 2 2007/2008	DATA COLLECTION 1 2001/2001	DATA COLLECTION 2 2007/2008	DATA COLLECTION 1 2001/2001	DATA COLLECTION 2 2007/2008
1 – Decide child needs to be looked after	2 hours	7 ¾ hours	8 ¼ hours	12 hours	10 ¼ hours	19 ¾ hours
2 – Care planning	0	2 hours 50 mins	4 ½ hours	13 ¾ hours	4 ½ hours	16 ½ hours
3 – Maintaining the placement (per month)	4 hours	9 ½ hours	4 ½ hours	13 ¼ hours	8 ½ hours	22 ¾ hours
4 – Return home (exit care)					10 ½ hours	30 hours
5 – Find subsequent Placement					3 hours	24 hours
6 – Review	0	3 hours	5 ¼ hours	15 hours	5 ¼ hours	18 hours
7 – Legal processes	14 ½ hours	10 ½ hours	64 hours	28 hours and 10 mins	78 ½ hours	38 ½ hours
8 – Transition to leaving care services					48 hours	8 ½ hours

1. Activity times have been rounded to the nearest 5 minutes

TABLE 3.11: Proportion of overall time spent on direct and indirect tasks across the eight social care processes for looked after children

PROCESS	PROPORTION OF TIME SPENT PER PROCESS[1] (%)							
	DIRECT CLIENT RELATED ACTIVITY		INDIRECT CLIENT RELATED ACTIVITY		TOTAL			
	DATA COLLECTION 1 2001/2001	DATA COLLECTION 2 2007/2008	DATA COLLECTION 1 2001/2001	DATA COLLECTION 2 2007/2008	DATA COLLECTION 1 2001/2001	DATA COLLECTION 2 2007/2008		
1 – Decide child needs to be looked after	20	39	80	61	100	100		
2 – Care planning	0	17	100	83	100	100		
3 – Maintaining the placement (per month)	47	42	53	58	100	100		
4 – Return home (exit care)	Not available	27	Not available	73	100	100		
5 – Find subsequent Placement	Not available	37	Not available	63	100	100		
6 – Review	0	16	100	84	100	100		
7 – Legal processes	18	27	82	73	100	100		
8 – Transition to leaving care services	Not available	59	Not available	41	100	100		

1. Times have been rounded up to the nearest 5 minutes

It was also possible to explore the 'time use activity data' collected for the eight social care processes to support children in need. Table 3.12 shows the proportion of overall time spent on direct and indirect tasks across the eight social care processes for children in need.

TABLE 3.12: Percentage of overall reported time on direct and indirect tasks across the eight children in need social care processes

	PERCENTAGE (%) OF OVERALL TIME REPORTED		
	DIRECT ACTIVITIES	INDIRECT ACTIVITIES	
		ADMINISTRATIVE TASKS	LIAISING WITH OTHER PROFESSIONALS
P1: Initial contact and referral	32.31	23.89	43.80
P2: Initial Assessment	49.62	20.30	30.08
P3: Ongoing support	62	15	21
P4: Close case	23.09	42.00	34.91
P5: Core Assessment	19.84	66.76	13.40
P6: Planning and Review: CiN	-	49.07	50.93
P7: section 47 enquiry	28.50	31.43	40.07
P8: Public law outline	-	58.15	41.85

Tables 3.11 and 3.12 illustrate how the time spent on the different categories of activities vary across the processes for both looked after children and children in need. The percentages in the tables do illustrate that some of the processes have a high proportion of administrative activities. In order to contextualise these figures the focus groups provided a helpful platform to discuss the issue of time spent on different types of activities. Frontline practitioners reported that while administrators do support the role of social workers, they emphasised the importance of high quality recording and write up of assessments, reviews and other case records. Workers noted the importance accurately recording the information that they had gathered as it forms the basis of decisions and allocation of services. Moreover, social workers noted that they preferred

to enter the information into assessment forms on management information systems themselves. Even where an administrator was available, workers reported that they were professionally accountable and responsible for the content and any subsequent decisions and therefore would enter the data for themselves (Burton and Van der Broek 2008). Conversely, frontline workers and their managers also reported that in some teams the level of administrative support had been reduced as part of structural re-organisations and that they no longer had sufficient administrative support, in these instances social workers were carrying out administrative tasks that were not related to the completion of assessments (for example arranging meetings, sending documentation to colleagues in other agencies), workers also expressed concerns about whether this was the best use of their time (Ward, Holmes and Soper 2008).

Table 3.12 outlines the proportion of direct and indirect tasks for each process. This, however, does not necessarily reflect a typical working week. It is unlikely that a social worker's day to day activity will be evenly spread across all eight case management processes. In many teams, the majority of their time may be spent on just a few of the processes, and a disproportionate amount of their time may be spent on Process 3: Ongoing support. Given that the day to day activities of a social worker in case holding teams may not be evenly distributed across all eight processes, it is advantageous to consider what proportion of time overall is spent on direct and indirect activities – analysis of the event record data provides an opportunity to do this analysis. Exploration of the event record data indicates that the following proportions of time were allocated to direct and indirect tasks during the research data collection period. Table 3.13 illustrates that over this time period the proportion of time spent on administrative activities was 23% with almost a third of the total time being spent in direct contact with children and their families.

TABLE 3.13: Percentage of overall time reported on direct and indirect tasks across the event record data collection period

TASK	PERCENTAGE OF OVERALL TIME
Direct activities	32
Administrative activities	23
Liaising with other professionals	17
Other[1]	25

[1.]   Other included supervision, attendance at court, referrals and discussions with other agencies and unstated

The percentages outlined in the previous tables highlight that there is not a straightforward distinction between the proportions of time spent on the categories of activities. Furthermore, given that there are variations in the roles and activities across different types of teams and that work on the different types of processes is likely to fluctuate over time to meet the needs of specific cases, this suggests that the statement that social workers spend 80% of their time on administrative activities (Herbert 2004; Munro 2011b) has been oversimplified.

The role and work of Family Support workers

Analysis of the questionnaire responses for the children in need study suggested that in some instances unqualified family support workers were carrying out some of the *case management activities* that according to policy and procedural documentation should be carried out by social workers (for Processes 1, 2, 4 and 5). This finding was also supported by information provided by focus group respondents in both the studies that focussed on children in need. There is evidence that intake and referral teams have faced increases in referrals and workloads but not in their capacity (Holmes, Munro and Soper 2010; Brookes 2010). In order to respond to these increases it is evident that family support workers were carrying out some social work functions to reduce the pressure on the teams. However, for the most part this information is anecdotal and in most instances, it is not possible to distinguish whether the processes or specific tasks within the processes were carried out by a social worker or by a family support worker. Furthermore, analysis of the questionnaire responses highlighted that it was not possible to distinguish or disentangle possible overlaps in activity. Given the anecdotal nature of the information and the variation in the use of family support workers across teams, a decision was made by the research team to calculate the unit costs based on the processes being undertaken by social workers, in line with formal procedures. The unit cost per hour of a family support worker is lower than for their qualified social worker colleagues (as a result of lower salary scales).Therefore, the unit costs outlined in the follow section of this chapter and later in the book are higher than if the processes were costed based on the activities being carried out by family support workers. The use of unqualified family support workers to complete social work tasks is an issue that requires further consideration in the future.

Chapter 3: Summary

- The cost methodology outlined in this chapter uses the time taken to carry out *case management activities* associated with the processes identified in the previous chapter as the basis for building up unit costs.

- Three methods have been used to collect 'time use activity data' for the processes: focus groups, questionnaires/online surveys and event records.

- Unit costs were calculated using these data together with information about salaries and overheads.

- A framework to calculate the costs of overheads using a consistent and transparent approach is introduced.

- The methodological advantages and difficulties of triangulating the data from the different methods are outlined.

- Variations in activity to support children in need and disabled children in receipt of short break services are identified.

- This chapter also provides examples of how the data can be analysed to explore proportions of time spent on the different types of tasks outlined in Chapter 2.

CHAPTER 4

Additional Services

Introduction

As detailed throughout this book, the costs and outcomes research programme carried out by the Centre for Child and Family Research (CCFR) has differentiated between the costs of activities associated with *case management activities* carried out by frontline social care practitioners as part of the ongoing monitoring and assessment of cases and those associated with the provision of *additional services* aimed at addressing specific needs, for example, placements for looked after children, therapeutic interventions or parenting classes. The two previous chapters have focussed on the *case management activities* and the focus of this chapter will shift onto the *additional services*. The recording of data about the provision of *additional services* is explored and worked examples are provided.

As outlined in Chapter 2 the distinction between *case management activities* and *additional services* was first made in the original study that focussed on looked after children. For these children once they are placed in care the core service component is the placement and therefore the cost of the placement is the most substantive cost element. However, it was evident that children also receive a range of different services, from a range of providers to support them in their placement, for example the involvement of Child and Adolescent Mental Health Services (CAMHS), services provided by youth offending teams to support young offenders, or educational support services. In order to fully understand the costs of providing services to vulnerable children it is essential to be able to include all of the services in cost calculations.

The original study highlighted that information about *additional services* was not usually routinely recorded on social care management information systems, particularly in a format that can easily be extracted for analysis (Ward, Holmes and Soper 2008). In order to explore and cost the services provided to looked after children it was necessary for the research team to examine detailed paper based case notes and use this information to supplement the data from management information systems. The case file data was not always comprehensively recorded and where possible, for a sub-sample of children a 'service provision checklist' was utilised by the research team in interviews with young people to ascertain the services that they had received. The 'service provision checklist' was a tool based on the CSRI (Client Service Receipt Inventory), to record type of services, along with length and frequency of attendance at the service (Beecham and Knapp 2001).

Children in need will also be in receipt of *additional services*, provided as part of their child in need plan. These *additional services* may be provided either by the same team as those carrying out the *case management activities* or by another team or agency (Holmes *et al.* 2010; Ward *et al.* 2008). Such teams are not necessarily case holding; rather they carry out time specific work with a family on an identified area such as tantrums, daily routine for the child and their family or parenting skills. In addition to services provided from within social care, other agencies or voluntary or independent providers may deliver a range of services. All *additional services* are provided in order to address identified needs and may be offered to the child, parents or siblings.

The provision of these *additional services* occurs alongside the *case management* activities as part of the interventions in place to support a child and their family. For some children and families, these *additional services* are likely to be provided as part of a package of service provisions, in order to best meet the needs identified (Department for Education and Skills, 2004). Indeed, the Common Assessment Framework (CAF) is designed to identify a 'Team around the Child' (or in some localities, 'Team around the Family') comprising professionals from a number of agencies providing support to meet the needs identified in the CAF. In Chapter 2 the timeline for Jack (Box 2.4) illustrated how the *case management activities* carried out to support Jack, as a child in need may be provided over time. Jack was in receipt of services in addition to the ongoing support. The timeline below shows both of these elements.

Box 4.1 Jack's story: Part 2

In addition to the support provided to Jack and his mother by his allocated social worker, a family support worker from the same team was allocated to his case. This worker carried out a focused piece of work to help Jack's mother discipline him appropriately and to help Jack control his anger. These issues were both identified as part of the initial assessment and the provision of the services was identified in the care plan. This piece of work was carried out over a six week time period.

Once this work had been carried out the family support worker and the allocated social worker had an informal discussion to examine how Jack and his mother were getting on. The activity for this discussion is included in Process 3: Ongoing support. It was decided that Jack's mother would benefit from attending an eight week parenting course provided by a local voluntary agency. Jack's mother started to attend the course in January 2009.

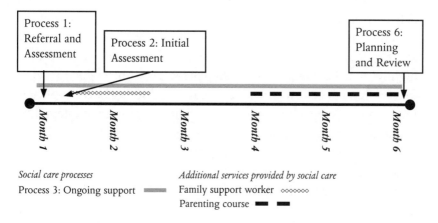

FIGURE 4.1 Timeline for Jack including additional services

The timeline for Jack illustrates how the two elements can be brought together to understand the interventions and ongoing support that are provided to a child over a period of time. The use of these data elements to build up costs and then use the data is explored further in Chapter 6. In order to achieve the aim of being able to explore the relationship between needs, costs and outcomes, understanding service provision is essential. To facilitate the inclusion of *additional services* in cost calculations and modelling of costs the availability of data on service provision needs to be examined. The following section of this chapter focuses on the availability of data about *additional services*, in relation to children in need and also discusses some of the identified key issues in terms of how the information is recorded.

Services for children in need

The provision of services for children in need is complex; representing a wide range of services and a variety of provision. A complex picture of *additional services* for children in need have been identified by studies undertaken by CCFR (Gatehouse, Ward and Holmes 2008; Ward *et al.* 2008; Holmes, McDermid and Sempik 2010; Holmes *et al.* 2010). These services include a range of service types, service providers as well as funding and delivery arrangements. Movements towards further integration between agencies and the services they deliver alongside authorities' responses to local need, have created a myriad of different *additional services* available to children in need and their families. The mapping exercise, introduced in Chapter 2, highlighted the complexity of the landscape within which services for children in need are provided (Ward *et al.* 2008). Current policy in England is driving a high rate of change in the process of integrating children's services within and across agencies, resulting in the re-drawing of the parameters of children's social care. These issues present both conceptual and practical difficulties when implementing a 'bottom up' costing methodology. However, such difficulties are not insurmountable. One of the advantages of such a model is that it offers transparency, enabling reasonable cost comparisons to be made. Consequently in utilising the 'bottom up' methodology to calculate the costs of support and services to children in need, it was necessary to define the parameters within which the research team should operate.

As noted in Chapter 1, it is evident from the data that has been collected for the research that the policy agenda of partnership and integrated working has been embraced both across and within agencies. A wide range of agencies may be involved in supporting children in need and their families. Those children with the most complex needs, and especially disabled children, or children requiring additional educational support, may be receiving ongoing support and *additional services* from a number of different agencies (see also Holmes, McDermid and Sempik 2010).

The commissioning of services has increasingly become a joint activity, particularly with the use of multi-agency decision making panels. The aforementioned mapping exercise identified an ever changing and expanding 'macro map' of service commissioning and provision that reflects the wide variety of service providers and partnership arrangements. Research carried out by CCFR has identified that the process of commissioning services is costly, both in terms of setting up new contracts and also maintaining contracts (Holmes, McDermid and Sempik 2010).

The task of listing all the possible support that may be provided to children in need and their families would be vast. As such, the research that focussed on children in need, initially focussed on the costs incurred to children's social care. The work undertaken by the research team does, however, acknowledge that the demarcation between agencies is a functional one, and additional costs may be incurred to support of some families. As such the research team have drawn on related studies to cost education services provided to children with special educational needs, along with health, and short breaks (Holmes, McDermid and Sempik 2010), and other sources, for example the annual compendium of health and social care unit costs collated and produced by the Personal Social Services Research Unit (PSSRU) (Curtis, 2010).

The picture is further confused by a lack of consistent definitions. Initially in the mapping exercise it appeared that all the participating authorities provided some common services; however, it later became clear that the boundaries are ill-defined. The analysis of the data showed that some provision bears the same name but offers different services in different authorities, and some authorities have different names for the same services. Furthermore, the research to explore the costs of short break provision found a similar picture with a vast array of services on offer across the three participating authorities. Even where a similarly named service does apparently undertake the same activity there can be variation and diversity. For instance, 35 different group activities for disabled children were identified across three local authorities. One authority provided five different after school groups, each working with disabled children with differing needs, requiring a range of staffing, running for a range of hours, each located in a different place (Holmes, McDermid and Sempik 2010). Indeed, statutory duty for local authorities to provide short break services, which came into effect in April 2011, states those short breaks must vary in order to meet the range of needs identified for disabled children and their families.

The sheer range of services identified by these two studies may be a response to needs led commissioning, with localities offering a range of services to meet the specific needs indentified within their own localities. This may be further compounded with policy moves towards even great independence for local authorities in decision making (Department for Education 2011a; Cabinet Office 2011). Moreover, the range of services offered to children and families receiving support under the auspices of the Common Assessment Framework may well become more convoluted. The range of *additional services* cited by the local authorities poses a challenge when attempts are made to cost services and make comparisons across and between local authorities. In addition to the difficulties in defining and categorising services outlined above in order to apply cost calculations to child in need populations readily accessible child level data is required for accurate and comprehensive cost calculations. The recording and availability of this data is explored in the following section.

The recording of services

The importance of understanding a child's journey as they receive support from a range of services in response to specific needs has recently been highlighted as part of the Munro *Review of Child Protection* (Munro 2010; Munro 2011). High quality data about service provision are required if children's services departments commissioning strategies and the assessment of outcomes are to be effective (Ward Holmes and Soper 2008; Department for Education and Skills 2007). This can be achieved through the recording and analysis of robust child level data about the needs of an individual child, or group of children, the services provided to meet those needs and the outcomes of those service interventions. Child level data enables analysis of changes in outcomes over time, making a significant contribution to the knowledge base on outcomes for children with different characteristics or needs receiving different types of services. UK child level data collections, including the SSDA 903 return for looked after children, and the Children in Need (CiN) Census, are internationally recognised as being robust and providing valuable longitudinal data on a number of key variables (Munro *et al.* 2011a). The costs and outcomes programme of research has, however, identified a number of key issues with regards to the recording of data on services. As in Chapter 3, this section of the chapter will use the study to calculate the costs of supporting children in need (Holmes *et al.* 2010) as a worked example to explore some of those key issues.

Previous research undertaken by The Centre for Child and Family Research (CCFR) has demonstrated how routinely collected child level data, such as those gathered for the CiN Census and the SSDA 903 returns, can be brought together with unit cost data, to explore the costs incurred by social care and other agencies of providing different types of child welfare interventions to individuals or groups of children (Holmes *et al.* 2010; Ward Holmes and Soper 2008). Research findings suggest that the best data on services is available where there is a clear relationship between the delivery of a service and a payment for that service, for instance placements provided to looked after children, short break services and direct payments for disabled children (Gatehouse, Ward and Holmes 2008). Data on *additional services* in the original study to explore the costs of placing children in care was routinely available for the 'primary service' for looked after children, i.e. their placements. Information on the type of service (placement), the service provider and the start and end dates was recorded in order to trigger the fees and allowance payments to the placement provider. These are also all key data items included in the national statistical return in England for looked after children (SSDA 903). The study to explore the costs of services to children in need sought to replicate this technique to explore how routine collected data could be utilised to calculate the costs of the services provided to children in need over a given time period, using the Children in Need (CIN) Census (Department for Education and Skills 2000).

The CiN Census was the first attempt to collect data on the numbers of children identified as being 'in need' (Department for Education and Skills 2000) and the services provided to them by local authorities. This was a biennial survey taking a week-long snapshot of the characteristics of children receiving social care services, the activity by Social Care Departments in relation to those children and the associated costs (Mahon 2008; Gatehouse, Holmes and Ward 2008). Prior to 2008, the last national data collection on all children in need was the 2005 CiN Census (Department for Education and Skills 2005). In 2008, the Department for Children, Schools and Families introduced the revised CiN Census to reflect the change outlined in the Children Act 2004 when Children's Social Care and Education Departments were merged into children's services departments. The subsequent revised Census has been designed to gather child level data which will make it possible to improve knowledge of the volume of services being provided to children in need and how patterns of service provision are changing over time. In addition, the Census aims to provide data for the analysis of support pathways of children, in particular those children who move in and out of the care system over time and the patterns of support they receive. The data provided will also make it possible to understand the costs of children in need services incurred by local authorities in order to inform spending and commissioning decisions at both national and local levels (Department for Children, Schools and Families 2009:3).

Local authorities submitted data for a six-month time period between 1 October 2008 and 31 March 2009 on the numbers of children receiving support, their needs and characteristics, and the types of services delivered. This was the first year of the revised CiN Census and subsequent data collections have been gathered for a 12 month period (Department for Children, Schools and Families 2009). As part of the study to explore the costs of children in need child level data were collected for a sample of 60 children across four local authorities (total sample size 240) for a six-month time frame to align with the 2008-09 CiN between 1 October 2008 and 31 March 2009. Supplementary data were gathered from individual case files (paper and electronic). The initial analysis of the service provision data focussed on how the information had been recorded and categorised for the CiN Census.

Holmes *et al.* (2010) found that it was possible to identify *case management processes* from the data gathered. However, the study also identified that robust and consistent data on the *additional services* identified was more problematic. It was evident from initial analysis of the data that the recording of some *additional services* were unavailable, variable or sometimes insufficiently detailed, inconsistent and sometimes incomplete (see also Ward *et al.* 2008; Gatehouse, Holmes and Ward 2008). The CIN Census was restricted to the collection of data on services provided or funded by local authority social care departments. Although the census collected comprehensive data on social care activity and expenditure, it provided little quantified information on the exact type of services being received, a point raised by the Atkinson Review (2005). Children's social care are now set within the broader structures of children's services departments; at least in theory, these have introduced greater integration of services, often underpinned by joint commissioning and shared funding arrangements. Data recorded on the *additional services* provided to children in need will need to take this into account and collect data not only on social care activity, but also on the activities of other children's services such as education, youth justice and health, that now work together at both a general and a specialist level to promote the wellbeing of children in need.

Examination of the data recorded as part of the CiN Census suggest that the fields defined by the CiN Census and the management information system within which the data are recorded do not necessarily reflect the range of *additional services* provided to the children (see also Holmes *et al.* 2009; Gatehouse, Ward and Holmes 2008). Workers reported that they are constrained by categories defined by fields in management information systems and in many cases social workers utilise free text fields to ensure the information is being recorded. As such, it was necessary for the research team to gather supplementary data on service provision from free text fields and additional documents such as assessments and plans. While it was possible to carry out this analysis as part of the research study, such an approach is prohibitively time consuming to enter and gather for monitoring and analysis purposes, at a local level and for submission nationally. The design of management information systems, and the administrative burden placed on frontline social care staff to record these data is explored in more detail in Chapter 5.

Where data were available about the *additional services* provided, start and end dates of that provision, along with the frequency and duration of interventions, essential for calculating the costs of provision over time, were inconsistently recorded. Examination of the accompanying case notes showed that in some instances the service start date simply chronicled an event, for example, the transfer of a case between teams. In addition, it was not always clear whether the *additional services* included in case files had been provided or whether they had been identified as part of a plan, but not yet accessed. Furthermore, from the detailed examination of case records, it was evident that the service types categories introduced in the CiN Census were broad umbrella terms which could refer to a number of different interventions (see Table 4.1). It was therefore not always possible to identify the specific type of service that had been provided.

TABLE 4.1: CiN Census service type categories

CODE	SERVICE DESCRIPTION
Y	Family support (section 17)
Z	Leaving care support (section 24)
A	Adoption support
X	Residence order support
SG	Special guardianship order support
P	Other care and accommodation
D	Disabled children's services - services usually provided by children's trusts, supported by local authorities and primary care trusts to meet the needs that children with disabilities and their families have by virtue of their disability. This includes social care, education and health provision
AI	Aids and adaptations

An analysis of the data with regards to the provision of *additional services* may be replicated across a range of other service areas. For instance, a similar analysis of the availability of service data has been undertaken as part of the study to explore the costs and impact of the Common Assessment Framework (Holmes, McDermid and Padley forthcoming; Holmes, McDermid and Sempik 2011). As noted in Chapter 1, as the Common Assessment Framework (CAF) becomes more embedded into practice, the thresholds between CAF and social care have become blurred and difficulties have been identified in the recording of services provided under the auspices of CAF. The Common Assessment Framework is designed to be undertaken by any practitioner in any agency, which may not necessarily involve the support or provision of services from Children's Service's Departments. Consequently children who may not be known to social care may be receiving support services as a result of a CAF. Studies undertaken by CCFR (Ward *et al.* 2008; Gatehouse, Ward and Holmes 2008) have found that local authorities have developed bespoke recording systems, but rarely are these linked to social care management information systems. Consequently, at present there is no way of measuring the numbers of CAFs being completed, the services provided as a result of those CAFs and their outcomes. The numbers, and costs, of CAF may well be underestimated. At present there is no universal or systematic system for recording CAFs, and emerging findings suggest that the number of CAFs being undertaken within localities may be underestimated. This may be rectified by the introduction of National eCAF, a management information system for recording CAF which, at the time of writing, is being piloted across local authorities (Department for Education 2011d).

However, Despite the difficulties identified above it has been possible throughout the research programme to utilise data from both routinely collected sources, such as the SSDA 903 return for looked after children and the CiN Census, along with supplementary data gathered from case files and other sources to examine the costs of *additional services* for children in need and within other services areas. While the example above demonstrates the problems encountered with identifying the data necessary for including *additional services* in cost calculations for all children in need, where data have been available it has been possible to include the costs of those *additional services* in the cost calculations. The following sections of this chapter use worked examples to examine how the costs of *additional services* can be brought together with the *case management activities* for the processes outlined in Chapter 3 to provide a more comprehensive understanding of the costs of supporting vulnerable children and their families.

The costs of services

Research evidence suggests that *additional services* are fundamental to the achievement of good outcomes for children in need, including the maintenance of stability for children previously looked after who have been reunited with their families (Wade *et al.* 2010). The provision of *additional services* may represent a substantive proportion of local authorities' overall expenditure, and that of other partner agencies (Ward, Holmes and Soper 2008). Moreover, in order to meet the demands of public spending cuts, social welfare policy is taking greater steps towards introducing a more mixed economy approach to service provision, including an increased use of the private sector (Cabinet Office 2011). Therefore, the onus on local authorities to explore how services for children and families can be commissioned from a range of independent and voluntary providers is likely to increase. The need to develop a more robust evidence base in order to more fully understand the costs of *additional services* to all vulnerable children and their families becomes increasingly pertinent. Thus, the method outlined in this chapter may be used by both commissioners when procuring services and providers when negotiating with 'purchasers' to introduce transparency and competition into their costs.

As outlined in the introduction to this chapter, Ward, Holmes and Soper (2008) identified that those children with the greatest needs are more likely to receive the most costly services. This finding has been supported by other studies in the programme with regards to the services provided to children in need and to disabled children receiving short breaks (Holmes *et al.* 2010; Holmes, McDermid and Sempik 2010). These studies have found that the children with the most complex needs are likely to require the most costly packages of *additional services*. Due to the high levels of training, specialist equipment and intensive levels of intervention required for children with the complex health or behavioural needs these services are often the most costly of those provided by children's services departments (Holmes, McDermid and Sempik 2010; Ward, Holmes and Soper 2008). In contrast, some children with lower levels of need may receive less costly but nonetheless essential services (Ward *et al.* 2008). Children's needs are explored further in Chapter 5. Understanding the types of *additional services* provided to individual children or groups of children and their costs can be used to develop a more comprehensive evidence base to support commissioning and strategic planning.

Given the important role that *additional services* play in supporting vulnerable children and families, understanding how the costs of these services build up over time and the factors that drive costs is essential to develop a robust evidence base. As with Chapter 2, the remainder of this chapter uses two worked examples. The first, based on the study to explore services to children in need, demonstrates how the cost of *additional services* can be bought together with the costs of the *case management processes*, detailed in Chapter 3, to show how a comprehensive understanding of costs over time can be obtained. The second worked example, from the study to cost short break provision (Holmes, McDermid and Sempik 2010) demonstrates how the costs of different types of *additional services* might be calculated using the 'bottom up' method, in order to more fully understand the factors that impact on the cost of services.

Including additional services in cost calculations

As part of the study to calculate the costs of providing support to children in need, it was possible to link the unit costs of the *case management activities* outlined in Chapter 2 to the child level data gathered for a sample of children in need (as outlined above) to analyse a number of cost case studies to explore the impact of different factors on the overall costs. Costs were calculated over the six month data collection period. Existing unit costs for different types of services from other sources (such as Beecham and Sinclair 2007; Curtis 2010; Holmes, McDermid and Sempik 2010) have been applied to data gathered about additional service provision. Where necessary, the unit costs of different types of services have been inflated to financial year 2010-11 using the inflation index outlined in Curtis, (2010). London and out of London costs were calculated. Using this method, it was possible to calculate the costs of the services provided to Jack (as outlined in Box 4.1 and Figure 4.1 earlier in this chapter). The corresponding service costs are detailed in Table 4.2.

The cost of the *additional services* constitutes 37% of the overall cost of supporting Jack over the six month period. Holmes *et al.* (2010) found that for children with more complex needs, this proportion of overall spend is likely to be higher. The costs of *additional services* constituted between 28% and 65% of the overall costs calculated for the children in the sample. It has been possible to incorporate some of the costs of services provided by other agencies. To fully understand the full costs to the public purse, comprehensive data is required with regards to the provision of services across all child welfare agencies (Ward, Holmes and Soper 2008); this is explored further in Chapter 7.

The costs calculated for Jack include those services provided by social care. As noted above, children in need may receive services

TABLE 4.2: Social care costs of providing case management process and additional services to Jack over a 6 month time period[1]

SOCIAL CARE ACTIVITY COSTS: OUT OF LONDON COSTS				ADDITIONAL SERVICES COSTS: OUT OF LONDON COSTS			
				Social care services			
Process	Frequency	Unit cost (£)	Subtotal (£)	Service	Frequency	Unit cost (£)	Subtotal (£)
1 - Initial Contact and Referral	1	*191.66*	*191.66*	Family Support	Once a week for 10 weeks.	34.54[2]	345.45
2 - Initial Assessment	1	*278.89*	*278.89*	Parenting programme	*Once a week for 8 weeks.*	41.18[3]	329.42
CiN 3 – Ongoing support	Six months	192.70	693.79				
Cost of social care case management activity (£)			1,164.35	Cost of service provision (£)			674.87
Total cost incurred by children's social care for Child A during the six month period							£1,839,22

[1.] Costs inflated for financial year 2010-11

[2.] Unit cost based on a one hour visit and 40 minutes travel time (Holmes *et al.* 2010)

[3.] From Tidmarsh and Schneider, (2005) inflated to 2008/09 financial year from a number of different agencies and providers. It is also possible to include the costs of services provided by different agencies to calculate a more comprehensive understanding of the costs of providing support to vulnerable children and families, as Eva's story demonstrates below.

Box 4.2: Eva's story

Eva was referred to social care in June 2008, aged six, due to concerns about her mother's mental health. Although both parents lived at home, Eva's mother was struggling to fulfil her caring duties due to anxiety and depression. These difficulties were also putting a strain on the parents' relationship. Consequently, Eva was assessed as being in need under Section 17 of the Children Act 1989 due to 'family in acute distress'. No additional needs were identified.

During the study time period, the family were in receipt of a number of additional support services. Weekly one to one home visits were provided by a mental health social worker from the early intervention service, a multi-agency support team. The mental health support worker was funded by the Primary Care Trust to address and support Eva's mother. Additional one to one support was offered to Eva's mother for an hour a week by the local authority family support team. The family also attended weekly group sessions at the local children's centre. There were two Child in Need Reviews during the data collection period.

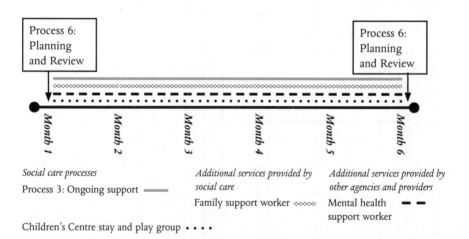

FIGURE 4.2 Timeline for Eva including additional services

The *additional services* provided by agencies other than social care constitute 47% of the overall costs of supporting Eva and her mother during the six month data collection period. Thus, it is evident that incorporating the costs of *additional services* into cost calculations, facilitates a more comprehensive understanding of the costs of supporting vulnerable children and families to assist in the strategic planning of services provided to all children in need. As services continue to become more integrated, including through interventions such as CAF, understanding the full extent of service provision to children in need will become more pertinent.

TABLE 4.3: The social care costs of providing case management process and additional services to Eva in a six month period[1]

SOCIAL CARE ACTIVITY COSTS: LONDON COSTS			
Process	*Frequency*	*Unit cost (£)*	*Sub total (£)*
CiN3 – Ongoing support	6 months	192.70	1,156.19
CiN6 – Planning and Review	2 months	276.23	552.45
Cost of social care case management activity (£)			1,708.64

ADDITIONAL SERVICES COSTS: LONDON COSTS				
Social care services				
Service	*Frequency*		*Unit cost (£)*	*Sub total (£)*
Family Support	Once a week for 21 weeks[2].		43.63	916.13
(£)				916.13
Services from other agencies				
Service	*Provider*	*Frequency*	*Unit cost (£)*	*Sub total (£)*
Children's centre stay and play group	Local authority, not social care	Once a week for 21 weeks[3]	14.83	311.49
One to one support from mental health social worker	Health	Once a week for 21 weeks[4]	95.95	2,014.96
Cost of service provision from other providers (£)				2,326.45

Total cost incurred by children's social care for Eva during the 6-month period	**£2,624.77**
Total cost incurred for Eva during the 6-month period	**£4,951.22**

[1.] Costs inflated for financial year 2010-11
[2.] Unit cost based on a one hour visit and 40 minutes travel time.
[3.] From Tidmarsh and Schneider (2005) inflated to financial year 2010-11.
[4.] From Curtis (2007) P.116 inflated to financial year 2010-11.

Calculating the costs of additional services

The aforementioned study to cost short break services provided to disabled children and their families calculated the unit costs of different types of short break services. The study aimed to identify variations in the costs of those services and the factors that affect those costs. Disabled children are not a homogenous group (McDermid *et al.* 2011; Munro 2011b) and any one local authority may be providing services to children with a wide range of impairments, needs and personal circumstances. For many families, the needs of their child may be complex. These families may require high levels of support including specialist services, professionals with specific skills (such as the use of feeding tubes or communication techniques), or specialist equipment and adaptations to homes or community locations to improve access. Children with the highest level of need may require one to one, or two to one support, either in the home, at groups or residential locations. These services are likely to be some of the most costly delivered by children's services departments. Conversely, some disabled children will require lower levels of service intervention. In some cases their needs can primarily be met through universal services with some additional support provided to help them access that provision. For example, the provision of a worker to assist with lifting in and out of a local swimming pool, or a youth group with a higher staff ratio to account for the disabilities of the children attending may be sufficient for some families to maintain family stability and achieve good outcomes for the child.

In order to meet this diverse range of needs, all local authorities are required to provide a wide range of short break services for disabled children and their families (Department for Education 2011b). As noted above, such a complex assortment of *additional services* may make comparing the costs of different types of services for a particular group of children, such as short breaks for disabled children, equally complex. However, the utilisation of a 'bottom up' methodology enables the variation in costs between different types of services to be identified. The method introduces transparency into cost calculation so that the reasons for variations can be explored in more depth. Consequently, where possible, 'bottom up' costs were calculated for the short break services provided in the three local authorities participating in the research.

When calculating the unit costs of the various types of short break provision, it was first necessary to identify the types of provision available in the three authorities participating in the study. The research team constructed a mapping template based on a framework developed in an earlier study (Ward *et al.* 2008). The framework was designed to capture comprehensive information in relation to all the short break services that were provided in each authority. A variety of services were identified; each of the local authorities emphasised the importance of responding to local need. As a result the services were wide ranging. However, a number of similarities were identified, which made it possible to identify a set of generic service types for use in making cost comparisons.

For each service, information was gathered about the number of hours that the service was delivered for (including any additional time for travel, set up and set down), the number and type of staff employed to run the service and the number of children attending. Salary and overhead data were gathered in order to calculate the hourly rate for each worker involved in the delivery of the service, using the same methodology as outlined in Chapter 3. The hourly rate was then multiplied by the number of hours each worker contributes to the service. The cost per child can then be calculated by dividing the total cost by the number of children attending. Table 4.3 provides an example calculation to cost an after school club provision for disabled children.

TABLE 4.4: 'Bottom up' calculations of an after school club for disabled children[1]

SERVICE	STAFF TYPE	HOURLY RATE (£)	HOURS OF WORK PER STAFF PER SESSION	COST PER SESSION (£)
Afterschool club	Team Leader	£36.50	½[2]	£18.25
	Family Support worker	£19.38	3[3]	£58.15
	Family Support worker	£19.38	3[3]	£58.15
	Total cost per session			£134.55
	Attendance			**Cost per person (£)**
	Average Attendance		8	£16.82
	Capacity		10	£13.45

[1] Costs inflated for financial year 2010-11
[2] This figure includes the management, supervision and planning time offered by the team leader
[3] This figure includes: 1 ½ hours for the session, 30 mins to set up and set down and 30 mins travel

As Table 4.4 shows the 'bottom up' methodology enables the data to be calculated based on a number of different variables. For instance, this after school club has a capacity of ten children but does not always have ten children attending. The average attendance for the group is eight children per session. It is therefore possible to explore the different costs per child that result from changing attendance levels. This flexibility in cost calculations enables different types of analysis to be carried out to inform planning and commission. For example, it may be possible to explore how some services may be made more efficient, through the maximisation of capacity (McDermid *et al.* 2011).

Furthermore, the study identified a range of unit costs within each service type. Most notably, the cost of residential overnight short breaks was found to range from £71.91 per night per child to £383.35 per night per child. In part, these variations were a result of the different salaries paid and overheads levels calculated within each of the participating local authorities. In addition, the 'bottom up' methodology enabled two key costs drivers to be identified as determining variations in the unit costs of short break provision: the number of staff per shift and maximum capacity. These can be expressed as the 'adult to child ratio'. As noted above, research has found that short break services are delivered to children with a diverse range of needs, and services require some degree of flexibility in order to meet those needs (McDermid *et al.* 2011). The flexibility of the 'bottom up' approach also enables an analysis of services provided to children with different types of needs. Providing a suitable adult to child ratio is essential in ensuring that a high quality and safe service is delivered. Although there are currently no minimum standards for service delivery specifically for short break provision, local authorities and providers operate under the regulations provided for looked after children (McCann 2009), such as the National Minimum Standards for Children's Homes (Department of Health 2002) for residential overnight short break provision. Standard 30.2 of this document, states that providers (including local authorities) must ensure that staffing is sufficient to meet the needs of the children being accommodated. Some disabled children with the most complex levels of need may require an additional worker to be present at a residential overnight short break service to facilitate the best possible care for that child. This may increase the average overall cost for the nights that the additional worker is present. Furthermore, as a result the service that provides residential overnights for children with the most complex needs may have a higher unit cost compared to a provider delivering a comparable service to children with less complex needs and therefore requiring fewer workers. Moreover, as children with different levels of need access a residential overnight short break, the costs of that service may fluctuate over time.

In recognition of the different staff ratios required for children with variations in need, the 'bottom up' approach made it possible to calculate two costs for a number of the residential short break services: a standard cost calculated based on the typical staff ratio; and an enhanced cost based on the provision of one additional worker. The average standard cost for residential overnight provision across the three participating authorities was calculated to be £209.59

compared to £276.37 for the enhanced cost. This approach could be used across a number of services and providers to introduce transparency into cost calculations and to ensure that reasonable comparisons between services can be made.

This example demonstrates the complexity of calculating costs for short break services for disabled children. The 'bottom up' approach enables some of those complexities to be identified and explored. The overhead framework outlined in Chapter 3 is designed to introduce transparency into cost calculations, enabling a more accurate comparison of different types of services. Likewise, a 'bottom up' costing of *additional services* introduces the same level of transparency into cost calculations and therefore help to secure a more robust evidence base for commissioning and planning services, Thus making it possible to understand how the costs of different types of service have been built up and the causes of variations in cost. Such a 'bottom up' method contributes to a more robust evidence base for the planning and commissioning of services (explored further in Chapter 6).

This chapter also demonstrates how the costs of *additional services* can vary according to the needs and circumstances of vulnerable children and families. The influence of children's needs and circumstances on costs are explored further in Chapter 5.

Chapter 4: Summary

- This chapter highlights the complex nature of both identifying the types of *additional services* provided to vulnerable children and families and recording which services have been provided to them.

- Despite the complexities of recording *additional service* provision, use can be made of routinely collected national statistical data sets to facilitate the calculation of the costs of the services provided to individual children.

- A 'bottom up' approach to calculating the costs of different types of services and those provided to children with different types of need, facilitates transparent and comprehensive analysis of costs. Such data could be used to enhance an evidence base to support the commissioning and planning of services for both commissioners and providers.

- Combining costs data on both *case management activities* and *additional services* facilitates an exploration of the proportion of overall costs on the different elements. It is also possible to explore proportions of costs between and across a range of agencies.

CHAPTER 5

Understanding Children's Needs and Outcomes

Introduction

The previous chapters of this book have focussed on the development of a research methodology, how that can be conceptualised and the calculation of unit costs of both support and services. As outlined in Chapter 1, a key element of the approach is to better understand the relationship between the costs of services, the needs of children and the outcomes that can be achieved. Furthermore, how that information can then be used to plan future service provision and improve outcomes for vulnerable children. This chapter outlines the policy context in England of understanding, measuring and recording children's needs and their outcomes. Examples are used from the research to cost services for all children in need to illustrate how children's journeys can be better understood when it is possible to link costs, with needs and outcomes.

Background

Children's social care in England is predicated on a cycle of assessment, provision and review. Children's needs are identified through systematic assessments; services are provided in order to meet those needs and the services are regularly reviewed in order establish whether they are meeting the needs identified in the assessment and achieving the desired outcomes (Department of Health, Department of Education and Employment and the Home Office 2000; Rowlands 2011). This cycle is applied throughout all components of children's social care working with children and families either looked after, or identified as being in need. The Common Assessment Framework seeks to replicate that cycle with vulnerable children and families (Holmes, McDermid and Soper 2011; Children's Workforce Development Council 2009). The Common Assessment Framework is a tool to assess whether a child or their family has additional needs and a team of practitioners, across a range of agencies - the 'Team around the Child' (referred to as the Team around the Family in some authorities) group are brought together to both deliver the services in order to meet the needs identified in the assessment and review the outcomes achieved by the delivery of those services (Holmes, McDermid and Soper 2011).

The 1989 Children Act emphasises the identification of children's needs as central to service delivery. Rowlands (2011) observes that 'the 1989 legislation uses the concept of need as the arbiter for the provision of services' (p2) whereby all children and families are provided with services that are most suitable to meet those needs. Child centred approaches have been adopted, whereby the child is placed at the centre of service provision and a number of agencies work together in order to use their various expertise to most effectively meet the child's needs (Department for Education and Skills 2004).

In recent years the policy emphasis has shifted towards outcomes and the need to measure whether the services provided to children and families are meeting their needs. This shift was consolidated with the publication of *Every Child Matters* (Department for Education and Skills 2004) which emphasised the need for all services working with vulnerable children and families to work towards an agreed set of outcomes structured around five key areas: *Being healthy, staying safe, enjoying and achieving, making a positive contribution and achieving economic wellbeing.* While Every Child Matters has been reviewed by the Conservative-Liberal Democrat coalition government since election in 2010 and no longer reflects current government policy, the paradigm of outcomes focussed working remains part of the lexicon of the children's workforce.

The election of the New Labour government in 1997 bought with it the need for government bodies to be held accountable for their spending (Felton 2005; Burton and van der Broek 2008; Rowlands 2011). Public money was expected to achieve measurable improvements for citizens, which required goals to be objectively articulated and measured (Rowlands 2011). Performance indicators (calculated using routinely collected data that all local authorities in England are required to provide to central government) are used to routinely assess the functioning of children's services departments. The success of welfare spending in achieving its goals became of increased importance after the election of the Coalition government, and the substantive public spending cuts introduced in 2010. The Spending Review statement in October 2010 noted that the UK had, at £109bn, the largest structural budget deficit in Europe (HM Treasury 2010). The statement went on to explain that the implication of this for local government was 'an unavoidably challenging settlement' with 'overall savings in funding to councils of 7.1% a year for four years'. At a time of substantive public spending cuts, it is essential to assess whether public spending on services to support children and families are meeting the needs of those families, achieving positive outcomes, and providing cost effectiveness. The efficacy and outcomes achieved by services became a salient point as local authorities have had to make difficult decisions about how best to distribute diminishing resources, without substantially impacting the quality of service provision.

The original study outlined in earlier chapters to explore the link between the needs, costs and outcomes of looked after children (Ward, Holmes and Soper 2008) identified that the costs of looking after children varied according to their needs. This, along with the centrality of the cycle of assessment, provision and review within children's services in England, means that an understanding of needs and outcomes and their relationship with the costs of providing services is central to developing a robust evidence base.

Measuring children's needs

The aforementioned study to calculate the costs of placing children in care found it was possible to identify the specific needs and characteristics of children for whom a greater cost was incurred. The original study identified 11 needs groups, ranging from children with no evidence of additional needs, to children with a combination of needs, for example emotional or behavioural difficulties as well as offending behaviour (Ward, Holmes and Soper, 2008). Policy programmes such as Quality Protects (Department of Health 2000) stress the importance of local authorities assessing the specific needs of the children in need population in their area prior to planning and commissioning appropriate services. Policy imperatives towards providing child centred approaches to service delivery require a clear and accurate understanding of the needs of children receiving those services (Department for Children, Schools and Families 2007). However, evidence suggests that the understanding of those children's needs across policy and practice is less robust (Janzon and Sinclair 2002; Preston-Shoot and Wigley 2005; Axford *et al.* 2009).

Local authorities' management information systems (MIS) record the events and activities associated with providing support and services for children in need. Much of this information is routinely collected and processed as part of the Children in Need (CiN) Census (Department for Children, Schools and Families 2009), and other national statistical returns, and can be electronically extracted relatively easily. MIS are also used as electronic case records and hold additional information about to the day to day management of cases, such as diary notes, and any related documentation, such as assessments, plans and the minutes of meetings. The Children in Need Census identifies eight specific categories of need: abuse or neglect, child's disability or illness, parental disability or illness, family in acute distress, family dysfunction, socially unacceptable behaviour, low income, absent parenting (Department for Children, Schools and Families 2009).

At the commencement of the child level data collection for the study to explore the costs of children in need, the research team anticipated that categories of need would be identifiable from routinely collected data held on management information systems and submitted to central government as part of the Children in Need Census. However, the indications from the study suggest that defining and recording the range of needs presented by this population of children is a complex task. The research carried out by CCFR suggests that the categories used by management information systems do not necessarily accurately reflect practitioner's conceptualisations of need (Holmes *et al.* 2010), which may be less well defined, may be categorised using multiple CiN Census categories, may change over time for a single case, and may be more closely linked with assessments of severity of need rather than type of need.

Percy-Smith, (1992) highlights the importance for practitioners and service users to be involved in the process of defining needs categories. Therefore participants in the focus groups as part of the study to explore the costs of supporting children in need were consulted on the types of cases which may require higher or lower levels of activity, and consequently costs. When asked this question, focus group participants made reference to children who had 'complex' or 'high' levels of need, although the specific type of need remained ambiguous. 'Complex' need was use as a 'catch all' term which could refer to either children with a high severity of need, such as severe learning difficulties, or children with multiple needs, such as learning difficulties alongside behavioural difficulties. Other categories of need identified by practitioners included: sibling groups; children with emotional or behavioural difficulties; children with a large number of professionals or agencies involved in their case; families with low levels of engagement in services; and children who move in and out of care. Focus group participants also observed that, as noted in Chapter 1, greater demand for services and higher thresholds had resulted in higher levels of need across case loads. Many social workers made comments similar those of a worker who observed that *'all of our cases are complex. If they didn't have additional needs, we would not be providing a service'.*

Respondents providing information from either or both focus groups and verification questionnaires/online surveys found it difficult to identify specific amounts of time for specific groups of children. As part of the questionnaires/online survey respondents were also asked to record any additional time spent on children with additional needs based on the Children in Need Census categories. Few respondents completed this section of the questionnaire and there were insufficient data for analysis. The lack of data may reflect the complexity of defining needs.

The majority of focus group participants reported that identifying specific need types was difficult. Reticence to categorise children, in part, reflected the social workers' view that each case should be assessed and supported individually. Similarly, the study to explore the impact of Action for Children short break services for disabled children, demonstrated the complexity of categorising children's needs and the tendency to view children individually (McDermid *et al.* 2011). Data were gathered for a sample of disabled children accessing short break services about the needs and impairments identified for each child. A categorisation of different impairments (some listed as mild, moderate or severe) was given to workers who were asked to state whether the child had any of the impairments listed. A complex picture emerged, with the majority of the children in the sample identified as having more than one impairment. A seemingly infinite number of different possible combinations were identified making analysis of outcomes by need extremely complicated. The study demonstrated the complexity in accurately reflecting the convoluted and multifaceted nature of children's needs. This complexity suggests that service provision should be built around each individual child, and as such a 'one size fits all' approach to needs categorisation is not always possible.

This was particularly apparent in examining the emotional or behavioural difficulties (EBD) of the sample of children in need. There are identifiers for EBD in the CiN Census: the primary need code 'socially unacceptable behaviour' and the disability sub-categorisation of behavioural difficulties (Department for Children, Schools and Families 2009). However, discussions with front line workers and examinations of case files showed that these categorisations did not accurately reflect the myriad of needs that might be considered 'EBD', many of which were not reflected in the electronically extracted data. Therefore, it was necessary for the research team to gather information about the emotional or behavioural difficulties (EBD) of children in the sample from the individual child case records. In the absence of a single, defining data item to distinguish children with emotional or behavioural difficulties, the following criteria were used to determine evidence of EBD:

- Type of disability recorded as BEH (behaviour)
- Primary need code recorded as N6 (socially unacceptable behaviour)
- Permanent exclusion from school
- Statement of special educational needs in response to emotional or behavioural difficulties
- Attendance at a special school for BESD (behavioural, emotional and social difficulty)
- In receipt of (or refusal of) mental health support (for example, from CAMHS)
- A recorded history of self-harming or eating disorder
- Diagnosis of EBD by a health professional or recording by social worker of behaviour (such as fire setting) consistent with EBD

Workers participating in the focus groups to calculate the costs of supporting children in need noted that a number of factors could affect the level of intervention in a case, such as the personalities or resilience of the child or family. For example, some parents of disabled children needed more emotional support than others (Flynn, Dudding and Barber 2006). Moreover, the levels of intervention required are continually in flux, and events and circumstances can change the level of support that is needed. For instance, children can experience periods of changing behaviour (for example, the onset of tantrums) which may require more intervention, or events such as moving from primary to secondary school can increase the level of support that is needed.

Workers also highlighted that activity undertaken was affected more by the severity of the need than by the type of need itself. For instance, the impact of a child's impairment or disability on their quality of life may be wide ranging (McDermid *et al.* 2011; Holmes,

McDermid and Sempik 2011). Impairments indenified by McDermid *et al.* (2011) ranged from extremely limiting, requiring 24 hour support and specialist supervision and equipment, to very low (see also Holmes *et al.* 2010; Holmes, McDermid and Sempik 2010). While the disability types were recorded on the management information system, the type of disability alone may not accurately reflect the impact of the disability on quality of life. The degree of need may be a better indicator of need than the category of need itself.

At present only the need type is routinely recorded on social care management information systems. Axford *et al.* (2009) note that attempts to capture the severity of children's needs through the application of objective measures, such as a measure of actual or likely impairment to health or development, could assist in a better understanding of costs and resource allocation, as well as improving the recording of outcomes. The categories identified in the focus groups are not routinely collected or recorded on social care management information systems. Focus group participants argued that the needs types included in management information systems did not accurately reflect the complexity of children's changing needs. Difficulties with the design of social care management information systems have been highlighted on numerous occasions (Scott, Moore and Ward 2005; Bell *et al.* 2007; Burton and van der Broek 2008; McDermid 2008; Broadhurst *et al.* 2009; Holmes *et al.* 2009) There are difficulties in implementing a management information system that marries the dual purposes of the management of individual cases for practice, which requires detailed information to be gathered building up a narrative and reflective the complexity of need, and routinely conducting other kinds of analyses for monitoring and planning purposes, which requires consistency and comparability. While the MIS exemplars/templates attempt to introduce some consistency in the recording of needs, the anecdotal evidence from the costs and outcomes research programme, suggests that these exemplars highlight this tension precisely because they do not allow practitioners to record additional information that may be vital to an individual case. As data collection pressures increase on children's services departments greater consideration may be required when planning data management procurement, in how the data may be most effectively utilised for both the recording of individual cases, and wider analysis for planning and commissioning without imposing an increasing burden on front line workers responsible for entering that data (McDermid 2008).

Costs and needs

Previous studies in the costs and outcomes programme have shown that variations in costs correlate to variations in children's needs (Holmes, Westlake and Ward 2008; Ward, Holmes and Soper 2008; Holmes, McDermid and Sempik 2010). The increased cost may be a result of either variation in the *additional services* provided or in *case management activities* undertaken with the child. These studies demonstrate that those children with the highest levels of need often require the most costly services. Ward, Holmes and Soper (2008) found that looked after children with the highest levels of needs, such as disability, emotional or behavioural difficulties, or offending behaviour were most likely to be placed in the most costly placements. For instance, children with higher levels of need may be placed with specialist foster carers or in residential units who are able to cater for their higher levels of need. Subsequent studies have also identified that children who are supported in their families (once identified as a child in need) with the greatest levels of need are also more likely to receive more costly *additional services* (Holmes *et al.* 2010; McDermid *et al.* 2011). For instance, due to the high levels of training, specialist equipment or intensive levels of intervention required for children with complex health needs, these services were often the most costly of those provided by children's services departments (Ward, Holmes and Soper 2008; Holmes, McDermid and Sempik 2010). In contrast, children with lower levels of needs may achieve good outcomes upon receiving lower cost, but nonetheless, essential services, such as those provided as part of early intervention strategies (Allen 2011a; Ward *et al.* 2008). The previous chapter demonstrates that the costs of one service may vary according to the needs of the children accessing that service. For instance, the costs per night per child of residential overnight short break services may be increased by the need to provide an additional worker for a child with the most complex needs. In addition, these children often require the most intensive and time consuming support from social workers.

Needs and social care activity

The study to calculate the costs of placing children in care found that the needs of a child may affect both the type of case management process undertaken, and the time required to complete a case management process. This section of the chapter will explore how children's needs can impact case management processes, using case study examples introduced in Chapter 2. Jack's story, in Chapter 2, outlined the social care activity undertaken for a 'standard' case for a child with no identified additional needs. Chloe's story below shows the activity undertaken for a child and their family with more complex needs, or whose circumstances have become more complex.

Box 5.1: Chloe's story

Chloe's family had been known to social care since July 2007 when Chloe and her three siblings became subject to a Child in Need Plan amid concerns about poor access to health care, parental arguments and domestic violence. It was recorded that the parents had an extremely volatile relationship, with frequent arguments, father's anti-social and violent behaviour, along with several separations and reunifications.

A routine review was held in December 2008. As a result of additional concerns about Chloe's father's escalating negative behaviours, a Section 47 Enquiry was initiated. Chloe was deemed to be at the risk of physical harm and became subject to a Child Protection Plan. Chloe's mother was referred to a protective behaviours class.

Amid concerns that Chloe's parents' behaviours were not improving a Public Law outline was initiated in February 2009.

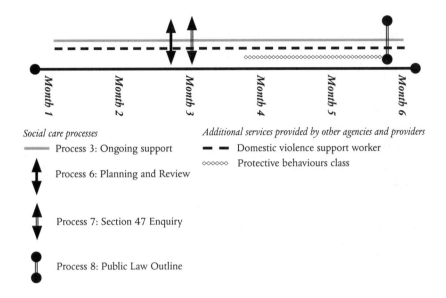

Social care processes

▬▬▬ Process 3: Ongoing support

↕ Process 6: Planning and Review

↕ Process 7: Section 47 Enquiry

❚ Process 8: Public Law Outline

Additional services provided by other agencies and providers

▬ ▬ Domestic violence support worker

∞∞∞ Protective behaviours class

FIGURE 5.1 Timeline for Chloe

As the example shows, in some cases, additional processes and therefore, more activity is necessary over a given time period to support children with more complex needs or whose circumstances have become increasingly complex. The additional concerns about Chloe's family necessitated an additional section 47 assessment (Process 7) to be undertaken and a Public Law Outline (Process 8) to be initiated.

In addition to the variations within different types of processes, children's needs may affect which processes are undertaken. The study to costs short break provision for disabled children calculated the cost of different types of referral and assessment processes by which families access the short break provision. The study found that each of the participating authorities had developed, or were in the process of developing, a 'tiered' referral process, whereby the assessment undertaken with families was determined by both the presenting needs and the intensity of service likely to be required. Short break services could be accessed via a 'local core offer' route for families with lower levels of need, and the traditional referral and assessment route for those with higher need.

The traditional referral and assessment route was undertaken in the participating authorities where it was felt that a family may have a greater level of need, which could not be met by the services provided in the 'local core offer'. In such cases a more in depth assessment was undertaken, most commonly an initial assessment. One authority was also using the Common Assessment Framework where appropriate. Participating authorities reported that a core assessment was only undertaken with those families whose need was greatest, and in most cases were only used when an overnight short break had been requested.

TABLE 5.1: Referral and assessment processes for short break by need

LEVEL OF SOCIAL CARE NEED IDENTIFIED	AUTHORITY A	AUTHORITY B	AUTHORITY C
	Referral and assessment route identified	Referral and assessment route identified	Referral and assessment route identified
Local core offer:	Panel discussion	No assessment needed	No assessment needed
Low Need			
Medium need	Initial Assessment	Initial Assessment:	CAF assessment
	Panel discussion		
			OR
	Total Cost		Initial Assessment
High need	Initial Assessment	Initial Assessment	Initial Assessment
	Core Assessment	Panel discussion	Core Assessment
	Panel discussion		
		Total Cost	
			Total Cost
	Total Cost	OR	
		Initial Assessment	
		Core Assessment	
		Panel discussion	
		Total Cost	

Two of the three participating authorities used panels in deciding how resources may be most usefully deployed to support families. In both cases, the panels consisted of senior managers from a number of agencies.

Table 5.1 summarises the referral process required for children with different types of needs in each of the authorities participating in the short breaks research.

As Table 5.1 shows, while there were differences in the referral and assessment procedures across the three local authorities, the intensity of the referral and assessment process increased in line with the level of presenting need.

However, as the previous chapter describes, research undertaken by CCFR has also shown that variations in the needs of children can affect the amount of activity time required to carry out the social care processes. Variations in the 'time use activity data' for children with different needs have been identified. For instance, the study to explore the costs of short breaks found that more intensive, and therefore, more costly, assessment and referral processes are carried out with disabled children with higher levels of social care need. Furthermore, the times gathered for the Planning and Review process for children in need differed according to whether the child was subject to a Child in Need Plan or a Child Protection Plan. Subsequently, the cost of case management processes for children with different levels of need vary.

The following section of this chapter explores the variations in costs for children with differing needs, and how these needs can be identified and linked with data on unit costs. As with the two previous chapters, this is illustrated using a detailed, worked example from the study to cost the services provided to all children in need. The example draws together the 'time use activity data' and unit costs presented in Chapter 3 with child level data that was gathered for the study.

Variations in costs according to needs: Worked example for children in need

As part of the research to extend the original methodology for all children in need, child level data was collected for a sample of 60 children across four local authorities (total sample size 240) for a six-month time frame to align with the 2008-09 CiN Census between 1 October 2008 and 31 March 2009. Supplementary data were gathered manually by the research team from individual case files (paper and electronic).

Given the difficulties identifying need outlined earlier in this chapter, the child level data collection was utilised to explore variations in case management activity, primarily that related to Process 3: Ongoing support between different types of Children in Need cases. As part of the manual data collection, for the sample children, it was possible to assess the level on ongoing activities based on a count of the number of data entries, telephone calls, meetings and visits recorded on the MIS for the six-month timeframe. Average times for each of these types of activities have been calculated using the 'time use activity data' from the event record data outlined in Chapter 3. Using these data, ongoing support (as minutes per month) could be calculated for the sample children[1]. This represents the sum of time

---

[1.] The mean level of ongoing support for all the children in the sample (n=180) was 5 hours and 30 minutes. This time represents activity by social workers and does not include that of team managers or administrators. The value is directly comparable to that obtained using event records. Using either event record data or data from MIS, identical results were obtained i.e. that social workers spend five and a half hours per month, on average, providing ongoing support for each child. The close agreement of findings from the two different methods supports the validity of this result.

spent per child on data entry, telephone calls, visits and meetings. Comparisons were then made between children with different needs[2].

One approach to explore the influence of needs on ongoing support activity was to examine the association between activity and the CiN Census primary need code of children in the sample. This analysis identified some variations in the levels of activity associated with Process 3: Ongoing support. There were very few sample cases of 'parental disability' (n = 2) and 'socially unacceptable behaviour' (n = 5) so results for these two categories were treated with caution. However, the socially unacceptable behaviour' needs group was associated with the greatest level of ongoing support with around twice the number of visits (19) and meetings (4) as the overall sample mean (8 and 2 respectively). Whilst the results suggest that socially unacceptable behaviour may lead to a high level of activity, although further analysis with data for a larger sample of children is necessary to reach a reliable conclusion.

Children categorised as having a need code of 'Abuse and Neglect' (n=75) also received a high level of activity with a mean monthly activity of 6 hours and 55 minutes. Children within this group received more visits (10) than the average (8) and visits (i.e. direct activity) accounted for 62% of the total activity. High values were evident for 'Family in Acute Stress' and those with 'Family Dysfunction', compared to the levels of activity associated with 'Absent Parenting' and 'Child's Disability' which were around half of that of the overall sample. It is possible that the low level of activity for disabled children could be accounted for by the involvement of other agencies (for example, health and education) that are also likely to be providing ongoing support and services.

However, as introduced earlier in this chapter, focus groups with workers suggested that the complexity and variety of cases, the severity of needs, and the resilience of different families to cope with a range of difficulties had a greater impact on the levels of ongoing

---

[2.] Statistical analysis was carried out using SPSS (v 17.0) and consisted of descriptive statistics detailing the demographics of the sample; the services received; cross-tabulations of ongoing support recorded according to needs groups and circumstances (e.g. the presence of a Child Protection Plan); and tests of significance between groups using non-parametric tests (Chi Squared and Man-Whitney U).

activity. Both focus group and questionnaire data suggested that, while the CiN Census categories were sufficient for the recording of cases, workers did not identify with the CiN Census need types as a way of understanding or measuring the severity of or complexity of need associated with additional activity. Furthermore, workers suggested that the needs of children and their families, and the level of ongoing activity required to meets those needs change over time. Furthermore, workers highlighted that the CiN Census categories for identifying the needs of children (including the Primary needs code, type of disability and Child Protection Plan Indicator) were not mutually exclusive categories. The manual data collection supported the view expressed by front line staff that the primary need code did not reflect multiple needs. Furthermore, the sample was not of sufficient size to examine all the possible combinations of needs based on the CiN Census need categories.

A number of other factors were found to be associated with increased levels of ongoing support activity: the child being subject to a Child Protection Plan (CPP); being aged under six; having emotional or behavioural difficulties (EBD); or a combination of these factors. The variations in the levels of activity according to these factors, either singularly, or combined, are outlined in the following paragraphs and are summarised in Table 5.1. Children with no identified additional needs were used as a reference group. The mean level of support for these children, with no identified additional needs, was identified to be 2 hours and 35 minutes of ongoing support per month (n=85).

Ten children in the sample had a Child Protection Plan (CPP) in place during the data collection period but no other additional identified needs. The mean level of ongoing support for children with a CPP (8 hours and 15 minutes per month) was over three times as high as that for those with no additional identified needs. This finding is consistent with results from other studies carried out by CCFR (see Ward *et al.* forthcoming). Children subject to a CPP had approximately twice the number of data entries, i.e. case recording entries and a threefold increase in the number of visits made to the child and their family. Visits accounted for 68% of the total activity time.

Nineteen children in the sample had evidence of EBD but no other additional needs. The level of ongoing support for these children (5 hours and 55 minutes per month) was almost twice as that for children with no additional needs. Analysis of the individual components of support (data entries, telephone calls, visits and meetings) showed a statistically significant difference ($p<0.01$) compared with children with no additional needs.

Analysis of the level of ongoing support indicated that workers carried out a higher level of activity for younger children. This reiterates the finding of Cleaver, Walker and Meadows (2004). For analysis, the children were separated into five age groups. Children under two received the highest level of ongoing support. Those aged two to five years also received more support than older children. Both of these age groups had significantly more ongoing support than those children aged six or older. Therefore, the two younger age groups were combined and compared with the children in the sample with no additional needs.

The total ongoing support (5 hours and 40 minutes per month) for children aged under six (but no CPP or EBD) was more than twice that of the group of children with no additional needs (2 hours and 35 minutes). Direct contact (visits) accounted for 62% of the activity time. Children in the oldest age group (16+) received less ongoing support and fewer visits than any of the other children in the sample. The total time for these children (2 hours and 15 minutes per month) was 59% less than that for the younger children.

The effect of combined factors on ongoing support was also analysed. A combination of being aged under six and being subject to a CPP resulted in total ongoing support activity time of 13 hours and 30 minutes per month, which was over five times greater than that for children with no additional needs. Those children received an average of around 20 visits per month compared with only three to four for children with no additional needs. Visits (direct contact) accounted for 63% of the total ongoing support time.

There were five children in the sample who were aged under six and had evidence of EBD but only three who had EBD and also had a CPP. Therefore, these groups were combined to investigate the effect of EBD in association with any other need on ongoing support (n=6). The mean level of ongoing support of this subgroup was 16 hours and 40 minutes per month.

The mean levels of ongoing support are summarised in Table 5.2. The differences associated with additional needs were calculated as percent changes in activity relative to that observed for children with no additional needs i.e. no CPP, aged six or older and no evidence of EBD.

TABLE 5.2: Factors affecting level of ongoing support (Process 3) provided to children in need

	N	MEAN TOTAL SERVICE ACTIVITY	DIFFERENCE IN ACTIVITY COMPARED WITH CHILDREN WITH NO ADDITIONAL NEEDS	PERCENT (%) DIFFERENCE IN ACTIVITY
Children with no additional needs	85	2 hours 35 minutes		
Under six (but no additional needs)	43	5 hours and 40 minutes	3 hours and 5 minutes	117.2
CPP (but no additional needs)	10	8 hours and 15 minutes	5 hours and 40 minutes	215.2
EBD (but no additional needs)	19	5 hours and 55 minutes	3 hours and 20 minutes	126.6
Under six + CPP (no EBD)	17	13 hours and 30 minutes	10 hours and 55 minutes	415.8
EBD + any additional need (CPP or under six)	6	16 hours and 40 minutes	14 hours and 5 minutes	538.9

Children who were under six and had a CPP or had EBD all had higher levels of ongoing support than children without these factors. A CPP was associated with an increased level of activity of 215%; a combination of CPP and young age showed an increase of 416%. The presence of EBD resulted in a 127% increase in activity, whilst EBD in combination with another need factor (aged under six or a CPP) was associated with the highest level of ongoing support, over five times greater than that for children with no additional needs (539%).

Contribution of different elements to the level of total ongoing support

Chapter 3 introduced the concept of being able to explore the 'time use activity data' to better understand the proportion of time spent on different types of activities, for example direct contact with children and their families. It is possible to carry out the same analysis of the activity data entries from the manual data collection. Exploration of the manually collected data entries showed that direct contact (visits) accounted for the greatest proportion of the total activity time (approximately 60%-70%) to provide ongoing support (Process 3) to children in need. Generally, as total activity increased in line with additional needs, all of the activity types (data entries, telephone calls, etc.) increased approximately by the same proportion. These data are shown in Table 5.3.

In general, children with additional needs or combinations of needs received more direct contact from a social worker than those with no additional needs. However, less time was spent in direct contact (visits) with children with EBD than with children in the other needs categories. For these children a higher proportion of time (18%) was spent liaising with other professionals. Hence, the constituent pattern of activity may be altered by additional needs as well as the total activity time.

Validating time use activity data for children with different needs

Using the approach of validating and verifying the 'time use activity data' introduced in Chapter 3 (Scenario 1), it has been possible to examine whether the activity times for Process 3 to support children with different types of needs are feasible. To reiterate the verification procedure makes use of average caseload data along with overall process activity times to explore whether it would be possible for social care practitioners to undertake all the specified *case management activities* in an average working week. Scenario 2 in Box 5.2 below demonstrates how the 'time use activity data' from the data entries has been validated.

TABLE 5.3: Percentage of time spent on different ongoing support activities

TYPE OF ACTIVITY	TIME SPENT ON ACTIVITIES ASSOCIATED WITH PROCESS 3: ONGOING SUPPORT BY CHILD NEED IN HOURS AND MINUTES (ROUNDED TO THE NEAREST 5 MINUTES)						
	All Children	No Additional Needs	Children under six	Children on a CPP	Children on a CPP + under six	Children with EBD	Children with EBD + one other factor
Direct contact (including travel)	3 hrs 25 mins	1 hr 30 mins	3 hrs 30 mins	5 hrs 35 mins	8 hrs 30 mins	3 hrs 20 mins	12 hrs
percentage of total	62.0%	57.1%	62.4%	68.2%	63.0%	56.2%	71.9%
Case recording	50 mins	30 mins	50 mins	60 mins	2 hrs	1 hr	2 hrs 20 mins
percentage of total	15.5%	17.9%	15.4%	11.6%	14.6%	17.2%	13.8%
Liaising with other professionals	50 mins	30 mins	50 mins	60 mins	2 hrs	1 hr 5 mins	1 hr 5 mins
percentage of total	14.5%	17.2%	14.0%	11.5%	15.0%	18.2%	6.4%
Attendance at meetings	25 mins	10 mins	25 mins	40 mins	60 mins	30 mins	1 hr 15 mins
percentage of total	7.5%	6.6%	7.6%	8.3%	7.3%	7.9%	7.7%
Other	< 5 mins	< 5 mins	< 5 mins	< 5 mins	< 5 mins	< 5 mins	< 5 mins
percentage of total	0.5%	1.13	0.5%	0.4%	0.2%	0.5%	0.2%
Total (hours and minutes)	5 hrs 30 mins	2 hrs 35 mins	5 hrs 40 mins	8 hrs 15 mins	13 hrs 30 mins	5 hrs 55 mins	16 hrs 40 mins

Box 5.2: Scenario 2: Validating variations in activity times for children with different needs

A full time social worker is contracted to work 37 ½ hours per week. Using the Personal Social Services Research Unit schema (Curtis, 2010) a social worker works 42 weeks a year, to allow for training, annual leave, sickness and statutory leave days, this amounts to 131 ¼ hours per month.

The average case load (for children in need cases), based on focus group data is 14 cases per full time worker. Holmes and colleagues (2010) gathered child level data on a sample of 240 children based on the Children in Need Census (Department for Children, Schools and Families, 2008). Using this data it is possible to estimate how an average case load might be composed of children with different types of needs. This assumes that the number of different types of children in the child level data sample is distributed equally across caseloads. A number of factors may determine the distribution of needs across different case loads, including the experience of the worker. Based on this distribution, an 'average' case load may be composed of:

Children in Need with no identified additional needs = 7 children
Six years and under = 3 children
Children on a Child Protection Plan = 2 children
Children with emotional or behavioural difficulties = 2 children

We can use this information, the activity times, and the variations in activity time for Process 3: Ongoing support according to need, to estimate how much time a social worker might spend on this process per month. This can be estimated as follows:

CHILD NEED	ESTIMATED NUMBER OF CHILDREN ON CASE LOAD	MONTHLY P3 ACTIVITY PER CHILD (HOURS)	TOTAL (HOURS)
Children in Need with no identified additional needs	7	2 hours 35 minutes	18 hours
6 years and younger	3	5 hours 40 minutes	17 hours
Children on a child protection Plan	2	8 ¼ hours	16 ½ hours
Children with emotional behavioural difficulties	2	5 hours 55 mins	11 hours 50 minutes
Total			63 hours and 20 minutes

Therefore, it can be estimated that on average a social worker might spend 63 hours and 20 minutes per month on Process 3: Ongoing support.

It may also be possible to include the activity for planning and review. If each case is reviewed every six months, then it can be estimated that a social worker undertake two CiN reviews and 0.33 CP reviews.

The monthly time spent on reviews can be calculated as:

Two Child in need Planning and Review meetings per month = 15 ¼ hours

0.33 Child Protection Case Conference Reviews per month = 3 hours

Total monthly time on reviews = 18 ¼ hours per month.

Additional regular activities can also be taken into consideration. Based on information from the focus groups, social workers reported that on average they spend 1 hour per month in supervision and 8 hours per month attending team meetings (based on a weekly meeting of 2 hours).

Each of these activities can be added together to estimate the time spent on regular activities per month:

ACTIVITY	MONTHLY ACTIVITY TIME
Process 3: Ongoing Support	63 hours and 20 minutes
Process 6: Planning and Review	18 ¼ hours
Supervision	1 hour
Team meetings	8 hours
Total	**90 hours and 35 minutes**

This leaves a full time social worker with 40 hours and 40 mins per month to carry out irregular monthly activities such as undertaking assessments, the Public Law Outline, closing cases, and undertaking other activities.

Applying variations to cost calculations

As outlined in the earlier sections of this chapter, both the CiN Census primary needs code and additional needs (being aged under six, subject to a CPP, EBD or a combination of these) were associated with differences in the level of activity for Process 3: Ongoing support. Differences between levels of activity for children with these additional needs and those without were all found to be statistically significant. Furthermore, such needs were some of those identified by social workers in the focus groups as being related to variations in activity time (more so than the CiN Census needs codes). Hence, these additional factors appear to represent more reliably the variations in activity and unit costs have been calculated as shown below. They have also been applied to the cost calculations detailed in Chapter 6.

Unit costs of Process 3: Ongoing support

The calculated times for ongoing support were used in conjunction with the average social care salary costs and unit costs per hour (shown in Chapter 3 - Table 3.2) to calculate the unit costs of ongoing support for children in need. These are shown in Table 5.4 and represent the monthly unit cost per worker for each type of child with the different additional needs (and cost variations) described in this chapter. Both unit costs for 'London' and 'out of London' are shown. Costs of the team manager were calculated from activity times determined through the focus groups and questionnaires. There is no evidence to suggest that these management costs were different for children with additional needs and therefore the same management unit costs were used for all of the categories.

TABLE 5.4: Unit costs of Process 3: Ongoing support according to child need[1]

CHILD NEED TYPE		UNIT COSTS PER WORKER (£)		TOTAL COST TO SOCIAL CARE (£)
		Social Worker	Team Manager	
Overall average cost (all children)	Out of London	158.04	34.67	192.71
	London	189.37	41.54	230.91
No additional needs	Out of London	75.08	34.67	109.75
	London	89.96	41.54	131.50
Under six	Out of London	163.05	34.67	197.72
	London	195.39	41.54	236.92
Child Protection Plan (CPP)	Out of London	236.64	34.67	271.31
	London	283.56	41.54	325.10
Under six + CPP	Out of London	387.24	34.67	421.91
	London	464.02	41.54	505.56
Emotional or behavioural difficulties (EBD)	Out of London	170.15	34.67	204.82
	London	203.88	41.54	245.42
EBD + one other factor	Out of London	479.61	34.67	514.28
	London	574.72	41.54	616.25

[1.] Costs for financial year 2010-11

As noted above, variations were identified in the type of referral assessment route for short breaks according to need. Again, making use of the unit costs outlined in Chapter 3, Table 5.5 shows how the costs of these different processes also varied.

Table 5.5 shows that the access routes by which families accessed short breaks in the participating authorities, on the whole, became more intensive as the level of presenting need increased. As such, the costs of the different process for accessing short breaks, while varying between authorities, generally increase as the needs of the child and their family become more complex.

Linking costs with data on outcomes

Outcomes can be defined as a measure of how well a child is faring on a range of components relating to his or her wellbeing or development. These components include: health, education, behaviour, self care skills, and social and family relationships (Ward and Jackson 1991). All children should have equal opportunity to achieve positive outcomes (Children Act 2004). Outcomes can be used to ascertain the overall wellbeing of a child, or may refer to specific outcomes identified through an assessment such as the Common Assessment Framework, an Initial Assessment or Core Assessment.

As noted earlier in this chapter, it is essential for policy makers and practitioners to routinely assess whether the support and services provided to children and families are meeting their needs and achieving positive outcomes (Scott, Moore and Ward 2005). Local authorities' commissioning strategies need to be clear that they are procuring the best possible services with their limited resources, and that families are able to access the best possible services to meet their needs. In order to achieve this, it is necessary to know what works, for whom and under what circumstances (Felton 2005). However, the measurement of outcomes can be a complex process.

Local authorities in England routinely collect data on the children to whom they are providing services. These data are submitted to government in the form of various national returns, such as the Child in Need Census (Department for Children, Schools and Families 2009), or the SSDA 903 statistical return for looked after children

TABLE 5.5: Unit costs of short break referral routes, by level of need[1]

LEVEL OF SOCIAL CARE NEED IDENTIFIED	AUTHORITY A		AUTHORITY B		AUTHORITY C	
	Referral and assessment route identified	Cost (£)	Referral and assessment route identified	Cost (£)[2]	Referral and assessment route identified	Cost (£)[2]
Local core offer: Low Need	Panel discussion:	12.36	No assessment needed.	Nominal cost.	No assessment needed	Nominal cost.
Medium need	Initial Assessment	315.89	Initial Assessment:	279.39	CAF assessment	191.27
	Panel discussion	53.56			OR	
					Initial Assessment	410.12
	Total Cost	369.45	Panel discussion	98.20	Initial Assessment	410.12
			Total Cost	377.59	Core Assessment	584.75
High need	Initial Assessment	315.89	OR		Total Cost	994.87
	Core Assessment	729.83	Initial Assessment	279.39		
	Panel discussion	53.56	Core Assessment	729.83		
	Total Cost	1,099.28	Panel discussion	98.20		
			Total Cost	1,107.42		

1. Costs for financial year 2010-11
2. Variations in practice were identified between the two out of London authorities, resulting in variations in the unit cost of a number of the case management processes

(Department for Education 2010b). These returns provide data on some key outcomes and provide a systematically collected national data set on all children and families receiving support from social care services. These data make a comprehensive longitudinal data set available which can be used to examine local and national trends. Recent research suggests that the national data in England is exemplary when exploring international comparisons (Munro *et al.* 2011a).

Much of the data gathered for the completion of the statistical returns are recorded by front line practitioners on electronic management information systems and then aggregated by managers for the returns submitted to central government. Concerns have been raised about the time required for front line staff to record the information included in national returns, reducing the time available for direct work with families (Munro 2004; Seneviratna 2007; Holmes *et al.* 2009; Munro 2010; Munro 2011a). Furthermore, concerns have been raised that in some instances, front line work with families have been driven by performance indicators, creating a 'tick box' culture (Munro 2011a 2010), reducing professional autonomy and skills (Burton and van der Broek 2008) and as a result having a negative impact on, rather than improving outcomes. For instance Skuse and Ward (2003) note that in some instances a small number of looked after children in England remain in placements that do not suit their needs to ensure that placement stability targets have been met. While aggregated data outlined in the national statistical returns provides an invaluable resource to inform the evidence and knowledge base there is evidence to suggest that the best use is not made of the data at a local level. While a vast quantity of data are often collected and collated by local authorities, some social care departments lack the resources, expertise and culture to support analysis and learning from the data for it to inform local changes and improvements (Scott, Moore and Ward 2005).

Furthermore, while the data on outcomes is gathered at the child level, a great deal is presented in its aggregate form. Understanding the different types of needs of vulnerable children and families, the services provided to meet those needs and subsequent outcomes is necessary to explore the effectiveness of interventions provided for different groups of children (UN General Assembly 2009; UNICEF 2009;

Wade 2010 *et al.*). As noted above, there is evidence to highlight that children's needs vary significantly, the needs and outcomes of individual children and families are also likely to change over time. Focus group participants in the study to explore the costs of services to children in need noted that external factors, such as periods of transition, for example changes of school can affect the needs of families and the outcomes that they are likely to achieve. Thus, child level data enables analysis of outcomes for children with different types of needs, receiving different types of services and can facilitate the measurement of changes in outcomes over time, making a significant contribution to the knowledge base on outcomes for children with different characteristics or needs receiving different types of services.

However, research has demonstrated that the measurement of outcomes at an individual as well as aggregate level in a way that is methodologically rigorous (Robertson *et al.* 2010), that best reflects the experience of individual children and families (Felton 2005), but does not place unreasonable burden on front line practitioners (Munro 2011; Munro 2010, Scott, Moore and Ward 2005) is a difficult task. A review of the literature about the impact of short breaks on disabled children and their families demonstrates that while studies exploring carers' own perspectives on the impact of the short break are predominantly positive, much of the literature using 'objective' measures is problematic due to methodological problems (Robertson *et al.* 2010). Such studies are indicative of outcome research which experiences difficulties due to lack of control on external factors, such as the provision of other types of services, the absence of a control group and insufficient sample sizes (Robertson *et al.* 2010).

Measuring the efficacy of individual services can also be problematic. It has already been noted in this chapter that children and their families vary enormously (Munro, 2011a; Munro 2011b). Service provision has attempted to address this in recent years by encouraging multi-agency response to services provision. A great number of children and families may receive a package of services, some of which may be provided to the child, some of which may be provided to parents or siblings (Holmes, McDermid and Sempik, 2010; Department for Education, 2011c). Consequently, where a number of services are provided it may be difficult to isolate the outcomes achieved by one particular intervention or service.

Furthermore, outcomes are not a neutral concept (Felton 2005). Practitioners and service users may differ in how outcomes are defined. For instance, in a study to explore the impact of short break services from one particular service provider, differences were apparent between practitioners from different agencies in terms of the outcomes that they sought the service to achieve. Practitioners from referring agencies defined that the principal aim and outcome of the short break was to offer primary carers a break from their caring responsibilities. In contrast staff from the short break services felt that the principal aim was to work with the disabled child to develop key areas and skills (McDermid *et al.* 2011). Developing an accurate measure of outcomes requires those outcomes to be agreed across all stakeholders.

Some difficulties have also been noted when measuring outcomes for children with the most complex needs. This chapter has already explored how costs can vary according to children with different types of needs. Those children with the highest levels of need often access the most costly case management processes and *additional services*. However, in some instances those children with the most complex needs appear to have the least positive outcomes (Ward, Holmes and Soper 2008). However, research undertaken by CCFR suggests that in some instances, the apparent poor outcomes for children with the highest levels of needs may be a result of the types of measures used for outcomes and difficulties in capturing the progress made by the most vulnerable children. For example, children with severe disabilities are some of the most vulnerable receiving services, with some of the highest levels of complex health, social and learning needs. For many of these children performing elementary tasks such as dressing, washing and eating are difficult. Progress may be small and slow compared to non-disabled children. However, given the levels of needs, vulnerability and disadvantage experienced by families with disabled children, the impact of small improvements may well be magnified. A great deal of support (and cost) may be required to achieve a small improvement in one of these areas, such as learning to use a spoon to eat. Achieving this outcome may have a significant impact on the child, their parents and siblings. In such cases, the amount of improvement made since the provision of a service or 'distance travelled' may be a more accurate form of measurement (Holmes, McDermid and Soper 2010; Dewson *et al.* 2000). Such an approach requires comprehensive baseline data to be gathered.

Felton (2005) argues that the impact of outcomes on quality of life should be taken into consideration and services' users involved in defining how outcomes should be measured. A recent report published by Ofsted states that too much focus is placed on checking that pupils are getting *additional services*, and too little on how much this support is actually helping children progress (Ofsted 2010). Outcomes need to be measurable, such as attaining qualifications or gaining employment. However, Dewson *et al.* (2000) argue that for those children with the highest levels of need 'soft outcomes' such as developing interpersonal skills or confidence may be more appropriate goals, although it is harder to measure them. However, the introduction of outcomes measures that are too varied makes local and national comparisons problematic.

Despite the difficulties identified in relation to the measurement of outcomes, it is imperative that costs are not understood in isolation and are always accounted for in relation to the outcomes they achieve for vulnerable children and families. The 'bottom up' methodology is designed to introduce transparency into cost calculations. This ensures that reasonable comparisons can be made about costs, needs and outcomes. For instance, the research that has focussed on short break services for disabled children has demonstrated that the unit costs of different types of services were greater for those services which provide a higher worker to child ratio. Ratios may be higher to meet the needs of a particular child attending a service, some of whom may require constant supervision or one to one support. A higher ratio may also be provided in order to achieve better outcomes for children, through more one to one time with workers. Thus transparency aids in the understanding of data: 'to understand outcomes data one needs to understand how the measure is constructed in order to derive its meaning' (Scott, Moore and Ward 2005:267). If data on needs, outcomes and costs are transparent and understood, they can be bought together to inform policy, practice and commissioning.

The limitations of routine national data collections have been outlined above, despite these limitations the outcomes data can be utilised alongside the unit costs presented in Chapter 3. As already indicated the original study made use of the SSDA 903 statistical return for looked after children, as such it was possible to identify differences in the outcomes for children with different needs and in different placement types (Ward, Holmes and Soper 2008). In recent years there have been modifications to the outcomes indicators included in the return and as such the resultant analysis has improved. These modifications include the introduction of the Strengths and Difficulties questionnaire (Goodman 1997) and improved indicators of the educational outcomes of care leavers (Department for Education 2010b). It is anticipated that as the SSDA 903 continues in the future and if the CiN Census is also continued that the quality of outcomes indicators will improve. With subsequent data collections it will also be possible to measure changes in outcomes over time thereby facilitating a more comprehensive analysis of the relationship between needs, costs and outcomes.

It is also possible to use the methodology outlined in this book to model various future cost implications of the outcomes of unmet need. As noted in Chapter 1, recent policy emphasis has been placed on the importance of early intervention on both costs and outcomes. There is some evidence to suggest that the development of more cost effective preventative services, which minimise the likelihood of needs and difficulties from escalating, reduce the need for more intensive and costly services, such as intensive interventions or specialist residential care, for some children at a later stage (Beresford 1994; Chan and Sigafoos 2001; Farrington and Welsh 2004; Axford and Little 2006; Ward, Holmes and Soper 2008; Allen 2011a). It is also possible to use the methodology to compare different service packages, or configurations of services for children with similar needs, such as comparing the cost of preventative services with the types of more intensive services that may be required for the same children if their needs remained unmet. Statham and Smith (2010) however, state that while the arguments for the potential for early intervention to save money have been popular among policy makers and practitioners, attempts to demonstrate this through empirical research have proved challenging. They further note that measuring the possibilities of saving involve a number of assumptions including the capability to identify those who would otherwise go on to develop poor outcomes and those who may receive a earlier intervention service who would otherwise achieve good outcomes if left unsupported (Statham and Smith, 2010). The study concludes that better data is required if reliable costs and effectiveness evaluations of early intervention strategies are to be undertaken.

It is also necessary to understand how a change in one area may impact on the outcomes within another. For instance, high rates of reunification can lead to high re-entry rates if children and young people are returned home prematurely (Scott, Moore and Ward 2005). Research to explore the costs of placing children in care has demonstrated that children, for whom finding an appropriate placement has been delayed, are likely to have higher levels of need and require the most costly placements. Furthermore, research has also demonstrated that the costs of *case management activities* to find suitable placements for children who have experienced several placement changes or have been moved in and out of care are likely to be higher when compared to children who remain in stable placements (Holmes *et al.* 2010; Ward, Holmes and Soper 2008).

Bringing together the different types of data, on needs, and costs and outcomes helps to provide an evidence base that can be used by social care practitioners and team managers to inform their everyday decision making and practice, along with commissioners and service managers, to inform the planning of services and distribution of resources within children's services departments. The evidence can also be used by other agencies providing services and support to vulnerable children and their families. In doing so children's services providers can develop a better understanding of the extent of need among children and families and the range of services required by them, the cost of those *additional services* and *case management activities* provided to them, and the effectiveness of those interventions, thus, safeguarding and promoting their wellbeing.

Chapter 5: Summary

- The chapter highlights the complexities of recording and measuring children's needs and outcomes.

- Variations in costs have been identified according to the needs and circumstances of children. For children in need variations were identified according to the child's age, type of plan (either a child in need plan or child protection plan), whether the child has emotional or behavioural difficulties, or for a combination of these factors.

- Use can be made of routinely collected national statistical data sets to facilitate the analysis of the impact of needs on costs and outcomes.

- Bringing together the different types of data, on needs, and costs and outcomes helps to provide an evidence base that can be used for policy and practice.

CHAPTER 6

Making Use of Cost Calculations

Building and Supporting an Evidence Base

Introduction

As outlined in Chapter 1, this book has presented a methodology to explore the relationship between needs, costs and outcomes and to provide an evidence base to support decision making within children's social care, and partner agencies. Being able to identify the different types of services provided to children, understanding children's pathways and how these relate to needs and outcomes for different groups of children, is necessary to explore the effectiveness of interventions provided for different groups of children (UN General Assembly 2009; UNICEF 2009). A rigorous and robust evidence base for child welfare policy and practice has long been accepted as being essential for an effective and efficient child welfare system. The application of empirical evidence is embedded into work that is carried out with children and families. It is used in practice and policy to inform the assessment of children and families' needs (Ward and Rose 2002) and the development of services intended to meet those needs. The green paper *Care Matters* notes that high quality information about children in need is required if children's services departments' commissioning strategies are to be effective (Department for Education and Skills 2007).This chapter will explore how the cost calculation methodology outlined in the earlier chapters of this book can be utilised to provide an evidence base to support decision making about the allocation of restricted resources to ensure that the needs of children and families are met.

Decisions about how resources can be most effectively managed to support all vulnerable children and families within a given locality can be complex, commissioners and managers may be required to balance a number of factors when commissioning services. Together with statutory duties, current government policy emphasises both early intervention and prevention strategies (Allen 2011a) alongside the recognition of the need for sufficient resources to support those with the greatest needs, such as disabled children (Department for Education 2011b) and those subject to a Child Protection Plan (Munro 2011b). Demand for both preventative and safeguarding services has increased at a time of economic austerity and public spending prudence. Corby (2006), notes that the need to provide both good quality preventative services and to ensure highly effective child protection services for those children at the greatest risk, increase the pressure to manage finite resources more effectively. At a time when an emphasis is being placed on both early intervention (Allen 2011a) and the quality of the safeguarding system (Munro 2011b), prevention and protection should not be seen as competitors. Rather, a strong evidence base is required to support decisions about how resources can be allocated across the children's workforce to ensure that resources are reoriented towards preventative services without child protection services suffering (Sheppard, 2008a; Axford and Little 2006).

While some children and families may only require short term support, such as that provided through the Common Assessment Framework, those with the highest levels of need, including disabled children, may require support and services over a prolonged period, and in some cases, into their adult lives. As highlighted in Chapter 5, the level of support required by children and families is likely to change over time and some children may move between the different types of social care support, or in and out of the thresholds to require social care intervention. The need to better understand a child's journey has been highlighted in the recent Munro *Review of Child Protection* (Munro 2011a). Furthermore, a number of children and families will require support from several different teams, services or budget areas. Therefore, in order to provide a comprehensive understanding of the costs and impact of a full package of services it is necessary to understand how the costs of different elements of those services, including case management activity and processes within agencies, build up, how they vary over time, and how changes to one area of service provision, may incur changes in costs within another.

As outlined in Chapter 5, robust, comprehensive and reliable evidence on both the costs and outcomes achieved by different types of support is essential to support the effective management of resources across the children's workforce, to ensure that the right services are provided at right time to meet the needs of a child and their family. Furthermore, effective resource management, will ensure that the decision making process about the types of support offered to children and families is needs led rather than resource, or cost led.

The 'bottom up' methodology outlined in this book is designed to provide evidence which can be used to inform decision making and planning to ensure that children's services departments can maximise existing resources without compromising the quality of the support on offer (Department for Education 2011a). The previous chapters have explored the various components that contribute to understanding and calculating the costs of both the support and services provided to vulnerable children and their families. The impact of children's needs on costs has also been explored. The cost case studies have also demonstrated that a number of these factors can act cumulatively to affect how costs build up for individual children.

Making use of the data

This chapter brings together those components to explore how cost calculations can be most usefully utilised to provide an evidence base to support the planning and commissioning of services, along with social care practice. Furthermore, additional cost case studies for individual children are utilised to provide examples of how the information can be used to explore the relationship between children's needs and the levels of assessments carried out. This chapter also introduces the concept of aggregating the data and how it can be used at a strategic level once it has been aggregated. Examples are provided of how the aggregated information has been used to improve understanding of the relationship between needs, costs and outcomes for looked after children and a worked example is provided to illustrate how the data collected for the study to cost all services for children in need have been utilised. The use of the aggregated data to understand a child's journey is also included.

Assessing needs, an example: Direct payments for disabled children

As noted in Chapter 5, the study to cost short break provision (Holmes, McDermid and Sempik 2010) identified that the level of assessment required for families to access short break services, largely, reflected the level of presenting need. However, the research also identified that this was not the case for children and their families in receipt of direct payments. The approach of providing direct payments has been introduced in recent years in England. The aim is to give recipients control over their own life by providing them with the funds directly to choose an alternative to social care services. As such the financial payment gives the person flexibility to look beyond standard services usually provided to disabled children and their families (Department of Health 2003).

The study found that in the participating local authorities, families with low levels of presenting social care need were offered one of two service packages: the 'local core offer model' or direct payments. The 'local core offer' was designed to assist families with disabled children with low levels of social care need, but who may need assistance to access leisure or universal services. (Department for Children, Schools and Families 2008; Holmes, McDermid and Sempik 2010). The 'local core offer model' offers the provision of a standardised package of short break services to a specific population of disabled children and young people, who meet an identified set of eligibility criteria. In two of the participating local authorities no additional assessment was required for children and families to access this provision. In both cases, the majority of activity to refer children and their families to access the 'local core offer' provision is undertaken by lead professionals from other agencies. Therefore, costs to social care per child are estimated to be nominal. Children receiving support as part of the 'local core offer' received very little ongoing support, such as reviews or visits, the level of which was determined on a case by case basis in each of the authorities. Indeed, it was noted in the focus groups that these children, having a low level of need, are unlikely to receive any regular visits or reviews from social care staff, although they may have regular contact from professionals from other services.

As an alternative to the 'local core offer model', families may opt to receive direct payments. These are payments made directly to parents or carers of disabled children from local authorities, which enable them to purchase services directly, thereby increasing choice. A family may choose to purchase for example, domiciliary support or a personal assistant for a few hours a week. In the participating authorities, where a request for direct payments was made by a family, an Initial Assessment was required. This additional assessment was triggered by the decision to receive direct payments, rather than the 'local core offer model'. As such the decision to carry out the assessment was not determined by the needs of the child and their family. As outlined in Chapters 3 and 5, the average cost of an initial assessment for short break services was calculated as £315.89 in London and an average cost of £344.75 out of London. As a result of having had an Initial Assessment, a family in receipt of direct payments was categorised as an 'open social care case' and was therefore subject to regular visits and reviews by social care practitioners, in line with the statutory requirement for children receiving support under section 17 of the Children Act 1989. As well as the completion of the Initial Assessment, focus groups within the participating local authorities identified additional activities to support the family to set up the direct payment and to complete the paperwork necessary to trigger receipt of the payment. Furthermore, additional activities were undertaken by administrative staff to monitor the direct payments and ensure that payments were made to families and were being used appropriately. It was not possible during the study, however, to gather activity data for this work carried out by administrative personnel, and it is therefore not included in the cost calculations, as a result the calculations below are likely to underestimate the costs of providing direct payments. Front line practitioners and managers of disabled children's services within the participating local authorities noted that this level of intervention was not always appropriate for the needs of some families, which may in many cases, were comparable to those families receiving services as part of the 'local core offer model'. Therefore the social care costs over time of two families with comparable needs may differ.

The following two cost case studies compare the costs of providing direct payments to a family compared to providing a comparable service to a family accessing short breaks through the 'local core offer model'.

Box 6.1: Jayden: Local core offer provision in a London Authority

Jayden was diagnosed with severe physical disabilities, and was referred to social care by her occupational therapist at age seven. Her mother was a single parent and had recently expressed concerns that she would have to give up employment to care for her daughter. As well as the economic stability provided through work, Jayden's mother was concerned that giving up work would leave her feeling isolated and without any adult interaction. Although the child and families' needs were primarily being met by universal services, it was determined that the family would benefit from some additional provision in order to prevent social isolation, and economic instability.

The case was discussed at a resource panel for short breaks. The family met the criteria for the 'local core offer model', and it was deemed that these could adequately meet the needs of the family. Jayden was offered eight hours a week home support from an independent provider. It was not considered necessary to provide ongoing support by social care professionals. The child's needs were monitored by the occupational therapist.

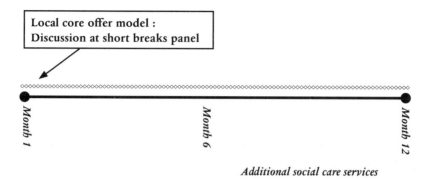

FIGURE 6.1 Timeline for Jayden

TABLE 6.1: Social care costs of providing short break services under the local core offer over a 12 month period1

SOCIAL CARE ACTIVITY COSTS: LONDON PRICES			SHORT BREAK SERVICES COSTS: LONDON PRICES			
Process		**Unit cost (£)**	**Service provision**		**Unit cost (£)**	**sub total (£)**
Referral and Assessment	Local core offer panel	12.73	Home support from an independent provider	8 hours per week for 42 weeks	18.56 (per session)	6,236.94
Ongoing support	None	-				
Cost of social care activity		12.73	**Cost of service provision for 12 months**			6,236.94
Total cost incurred by children's social care for Jayden during the 12 month period					£6,249.67	

1. Based on the costs calculated in Holmes, McDermid and Sempik 2010, inflated for financial year 2010-11

Box 6.2: Max: Direct payments

Max is a child with severe physical and learning disabilities living in a London authority. He attends a special school during the week and has two siblings, who attend a local mainstream school. Both Max's parents work during the week and his grandparents often help out with the three children at the weekend.

The special school and health services are working well to support Max's physical and learning needs. The family, however, have been referred for additional support to support the parents in their caring role for the whole family. The family have requested domiciliary support, specifically for assistance in getting Max ready for school in the morning and at the end of the school day.

It was decided that direct payments would be the most suitable form of support for Max and his family. Some activities were undertaken by the social worker to set up the direct payments, such as signing the contract and completing the CRB check for the personal assistant. A one off payment was provided to assist the family with the recruitment of a personal assistant. A personal assistant was recruited and attended a training day prior to starting with the family. The personal assistant was employed for 2 ½ hours each school day (12 ½ hours per week).

In addition to the direct payments, visits were made to the family by a social worker every six weeks and a case review was held every six months.

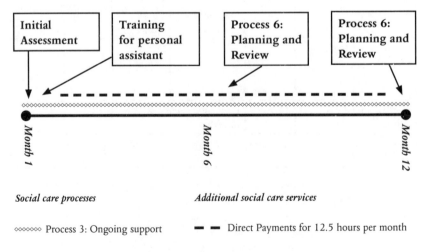

FIGURE 6.2 Timeline for Max

TABLE 6.2: Social care costs of providing direct payments over a 12 month period[1,2]

SOCIAL CARE ACTIVITY COSTS: LONDON PRICES			SHORT BREAK SERVICES COSTS: LONDON PRICES		
Process		Unit cost (£)	Service provision	Unit cost (£)	sub total (£)
Initial Assessment	325.27	325.27	Direct payments	12 ½ hours per week for 42 weeks 10.79	5,667.11
Activity by social worker to set up direct payment	365.07	365.07	One off payment to cover recruitment costs		52.91
Ongoing support visits	105.11	735.76	1 days training for personal assistant		86.36
Review	275.82	551.64			
Cost of social care activity		£1,977.74	Cost of service provision for 12 months		5,806.38
Total cost incurred by children's social care for Jayden during the 12 month period				£7,784.13	

1. Based on the costs calculated in Holmes, McDermid and Sempik 2010, inflated for financial year 2010-11
2. The costs of setting up and monitoring the direct payments are not included

Table 6.3 compares the costs incurred by social care of both the *case management activities* and service provision for the two different case study examples.

TABLE 6.3: The comparative costs incurred to social care of providing services through the 'local core offer model' and direct payments over a 12 month period[1]

TYPE OF PROVISION	COST OF CASE MANAGEMENT ACTIVITY	COSTS OF SERVICE PROVISION	TOTAL COST	PERCENTAGE OF TOTAL COST SPENT ON CASE MANAGEMENT ACTIVITY
Local core offer	£12.73	£6,236.94	£6,249.67	0.20%
Direct payments	£1,977.74	£5,806.38	£7,784.13	25.41%

[1.] Based on the costs calculated in Holmes, McDermid and Sempik 2010, inflated for financial year 2010-11

As Table 6.3 shows, while the cost of providing a service to Child A was £430.55 more over the 12 month time period, the overall cost of providing direct payments was greater and 25% of the overall cost was attributable to the case management activity associated with the case. It is therefore possible to see how the cumulative costs of social care activity and local authority procedures may increase the overall cost of delivering a service. Furthermore, recent government policy has emphasised increasing the availability of direct payments and personalised budgets (Department for Education 2011b). While procedures for accessing short breaks, including direct payments, may differ between authorities, it is evident that direct payments do require additional administrative and case management activity which may increase the overall cost of the provision. As the number of families likely to receive direct payments increases, consideration should be taken to ensure that the cost of obtaining, maintaining and monitoring the costs of such provision are as efficient as possible.

Aggregating costs

The previous sections of this chapter and earlier chapters in this book have demonstrated how the various cost components can be used to build up costs for individual children. While, exploring the costs of provision for individual children can contribute to an overall understanding about service delivery and a range of cost drivers, the value of the costs of pathways for individual children to inform decision making and planning is limited. In order to provide an evidence base for more strategic planning and decision making, the strength of the methodology becomes more pronounced when the data is aggregated to explore the pathways and costs for groups of children with particular needs, or in receipt of a particular service. The cost calculations can also be aggregated for populations of children, for example all children in need, or those looked after. The aggregated costs also facilitate comparisons between local authorities and assist benchmarking.

The decision analysis tool: Utilising child level data to model costs

When the original research study was carried out it became evident that the process of bringing together the different aspects of the data outlined in the previous chapters was incredibly complex. In order to account for the range of variations in activity, and therefore costs, and the variety of placement types the research team developed a model to incorporate the different data elements and to facilitate the analysis, by needs, service/placement type and by outcomes. As such a decision analysis tool (the Cost Calculator for Children's Services: CCfCS) was developed to bring together the unit costs of the social care processes with the child level data (Soper 2007; Ward, Holmes and Soper 2008).

The decision analysis tool is a Microsoft Access based software application that carries out calculations utilising child level data routinely collected within local authorities as part of their national statistical returns. The tool was originally developed to be used with the SSDA 903 data (Department for Education 2010b) on looked after children and was later piloted to use the Children in Need Census data (Department for Education 2010a) to incorporate cost calculations for all children in need. The looked after children version of the model has also been used to calculate the costs of Multidimensional Treatment Foster Care and to compare these with other placement types provided to children with similar needs

(Holmes, Westlake and Ward 2008). Furthermore, the looked after children version of the model has been utilised to better understand the costs of care leavers as they make the transition from the leaving care system (Munro *et al.* 2011b). The model has also been piloted for the set of education processes (outlined in Chapter 2) to support children with special educational needs (Holmes *et al.*, forthcoming). As well as being used by the research team, the Cost Calculator for Children's Services has been utilised by a number of local authorities in England under licence agreements.

For each child included in the data set the case management processes are identified as taking place using the dates recorded in the child level data and the appropriate unit cost for that process is included in the cost calculations. Start and end dates of services or placements are bought together with the unit costs of those services. The relevant unit costs can be applied where variations based on needs or circumstances are identified in the data. The unit costs are also linked with any outcomes variables included in the child level data. Costs are calculated for the individual child as outlined in the cost case studies included in previous chapters, and then aggregated in different ways.

It is the child level data that enables the various costs components to be identified for all the children in a sample. These calculations can then be aggregated in a number of different ways to calculate costs based on a number of different variables. At present the decision analysis tool can produce reports that calculate costs according to different child needs and combinations of needs, placement or service types or specific processes can be analysed. Different combinations of these factors can be explored, along with any outcomes data included within a data set. The model has a function to carry out a 'what if' analysis, which enables users to explore the cost impact of changing providers or placement types. It is also possible to forecast future costs of placements for looked after children, assuming that the children remain in the same placements. Costs can therefore be modelled in a variety of ways and the evidence base can be tailored to support different decisions as the need arises. In this way the application of child level data to cost calculations may be a valuable contribution to an evidence base to support decision making. The ability to configure child level data across a range of variables has significant potential in the assessment of outcomes, planning, and commissioning and localised practice (Gatehouse and Ward 2003; Scott, Moore and Ward 2005; McDermid 2008).

A further strength of the tool is that it makes use of data that is routinely collected by local authorities for national statistical returns. Children's services departments in England record and collect a great deal of data both for the national returns and in some instances for use locally.

Looked after children

The aggregation of the unit costs using the decision analysis model in the original study facilitated an exploration of the variations in unit costs both by needs and outcomes. The research identified that children who followed the least costly care pathways appeared to have the best opportunities for developing and sustaining secure relationships with adults and their peers. Furthermore, children with the most extensive needs, particularly those who displayed emotional or behavioural difficulties and were also known young offenders, were the least likely to access routine health care, and most likely to be excluded from school, to leave education without qualifications and most likely to be unemployed. These children with the more complex needs were also identified as coming into the looked after children system on average two years later than children with less extensive needs (Ward, Holmes and Soper 2008).

The original study also identified variations in the unit costs of different placement types, the average unit cost to maintain a child (per week) in a residential placement was 8 times that of the cost of foster care and 9 ½ times that of a placement with family or friends (kinship placement). These variations were as a result of both the fee or allowance paid for the placements and variations in the 'time use activity data' to support children in the different types of placements.

These placement costs have subsequently been utilised in a study to calculate and compare the costs of a specialist intervention provided to looked after children: Multidimensional Treatment Foster Care (MTFC). This is a specialist intervention developed for children with very specific needs (Holmes, Westlake and Ward, 2008). In a study to explore the costs of the MTFC pilots in England (MTFCE), the costs of providing these specialist placements were compared to supporting children with *comparable* needs looked after in non-MTFCE placements. The study showed a reduction in social care costs when children were placed in MTFCE. The social care costs incurred by the sample children in the first six months of MTFCE were about 15% less than those they had incurred in the six months prior to entry. The monthly costs of the *case management activities* to support children in the MTFCE placements were also substantially less than those to support children in residential placements, and on a par with placements provided by independent fostering agencies.

One of the key aims of MTFCE is to provide specialist foster care to ensure placement stability, and to support children and young people in care with the highest levels of need. The original study to cost looked after children identified high costs associated with placement instability and as outlined in Chapter 3 the study facilitated the calculation of a unit cost for each change of placement (Looked after children; Process 5), therefore illustrating how costs build up over time for children who experience frequent placement moves. The subsequent study that focussed on the costs of MTFC considered the costs incurred over a longer time period and identified that the annual cost to maintain a child in MTFCE (including the reviewing and planning processes) is around £73,121[1]. This compares with an annual cost of £65,4831[1] to maintain a child with *comparable* needs in agency foster care, £126,9031[1] in agency residential care and £161,5481[1] in local authority residential care (Holmes, Westlake and Ward 2008). In addition to the costs of the placement itself, when including the costs of additional 'wrap around support' provided by a range of agencies to meet the complex needs of these children, there was also some evidence that placing children in MTFCE can lead to a reduction in overall costs not only to social care, but also to other agencies such as education, CAMHS and youth justice. This is partly because the multidisciplinary activities of the MTFCE support team render the involvement of some agencies otherwise necessary for the higher needs children. redundant, but also because, where

---

[1] Costs inflated for financial year 2010-11

the intervention is successful, children and young people progress to a point where they no longer require some of the services (Holmes, Westlake and Ward 2008).

Children in need

As outlined earlier in this chapter the decision analysis tool has also been piloted to calculate costs for all children in need. The cost calculations carried out by the tool bring together the unit costs and child level data items outlined in previous chapters.

Child level data items such as the dates of Initial Assessments or Child in Need reviews, were used to identify whether the various processes had taken place. The child level data were also used to ascertain child characteristics so that the appropriate unit cost for a particular child could be used. Key data for the calculations are the dates on which cost-generating events take place, such as dates of referrals, start and end dates of assessments and case closure dates.

Despite the limitations of the data, as outlined in Chapters 4 and 5, it was possible to use a pilot model to estimate the costs to social care for a six month time period for the sample children (see Chapter 5 for further details about the sample children). Table 6.4 shows the average total cost per child in need over the six month time period. These costs are broken down by the four participating authorities.

TABLE 6.4: The average total costs of social care activity per child undertaken with all children in the sample over the six months time period by authority[1]

AUTHORITY	AVERAGE TOTAL COST PER CHILD
Authority A	£1,239.10
Authority B	£1,436.17
Authority C	£1,696.59
Authority D	£984.31
All Authorities	£1,339.46
Authorities A - C	£1,458.51

[1] Costs inflated for financial year 2010-11

As the table illustrates, the average cost for Authority was substantially lower than for the other three authorities. Authority D was unable to provide the same level of detail about children's needs and circumstances. In Authority D it was not possible to determine the data for some of the cost drivers outlined in Chapter 5: children subject to a Child Protection Plan and children with emotional or behavioural difficulties. Therefore, given the paucity of data on children's needs, the average cost shown for Authority D is likely to be an underestimate. This also highlights the importance of being able to easily record and extract data about children's needs and circumstances in order to facilitate accurate cost calculations.

Table 6.5 provides a breakdown of the average costs per authority by children's needs. The children who incur the highest costs are those with Child Protection Plans, or emotional or behavioural difficulties and another factor. For children in both these groups the average cost is more than three times the cost for children who have no additional needs (discounting Authority D for the reasons outlined in the previous paragraph).

One of the central aims of extending the methodology for all children in need is to explore the costs of interventions to children as they move in and out of the care system, i.e. moves between the social care system for looked after children and that for children in need. Many children in care will have received contact from social care prior to becoming looked after, and will receive support after returning home.

There were six children (n=239, so only 2.5%) in the study sample who became looked after during the study time period. Child 1 was placed in an Out of London authority and the remaining five were placed in a London authority. Table 6.6 shows the breakdown of costs incurred for these children over the six months time period. The costs calculated after the child became looked after are based on the original study (Ward, Holmes and Soper 2008). The costs have been calculated using the LAC version of the CCfCS and inflated to 2010-11 financial year. The costs incurred after the child became looked after include the social care activity to decide the child needs to be looked after (LAC Process 1), care planning (LAC Process 2), review (LAC Process 6), to maintain the placement (LAC Process 3), along with the placement fees

TABLE 6.5: Average total costs of case management processes for children with different needs by authority[1]

| | AVERAGE TOTAL COST OVER SIX MONTHS (£) | | | | | | |
	All children	Children with no identified additional needs	Children under six years	Children subject to a Child Protection Plan	Children under six years subject to a Child Protection Plan	Children with emotional or behavioural difficulties	Children with emotional or behavioural difficulties and another factor
Authority A	1,239.10	876.75	1,295.75	1627.89	3177.58	1,449.05	3314.12
Authority B	1,436.17	886.82	1,414.69	2,048.50	2906.93	1,457.26	3,085.76
Authority C	1,696.59	1,047.65	1,414.69	2,437.19	3406.84	1,723.79	3,349.82
Authority D	984.31	886.82	1,532.95	-	-	1,457.26	-
All Authorities	1,339.46	915.62	1,425.69	-	-	1,534.35	-
Authorities A - C	1,458.51	932.22	1,428.26	1,919.12	3160.54	1,538.40	3,299.86

1. Costs inflated for financial year 2010-11

TABLE 6.6: Costs incurred to social care for children who became looked after during the six month time period[1]

	COSTS INCURRED WHILE CHILD WAS NOT LOOKED AFTER, AND IN NEED			COSTS INCURRED WHILE CHILD WAS LOOKED AFTER				TOTAL COST DURING THE SIX MONTH TIME PERIOD (£)
	Time CiN	Average cost per month (£)	Total Cost while in need (£)	Time LAC	Average cost per month (£)	Total Cost while being looked after (£)		
Child 1	5 ½ months	198.08	1,089.45	2 weeks	9,826.45	4,913.22		6,002.68
Child 2	3 weeks	104.01	78.01	5 ¼ months	11,113.80	25,006.06		25,084.07
Child 3	5 months	98.29	491.49	1 month	8,301.37	8,301.37		8,792.87
Child 4	2 ½ months	615.92	1,539.81	3 ½ months	3,988.98	13,961.42		15,501.24
Child 5	2 ½ months	316.83	728.73	3 ½ months	3,752.95	13,135.32		13,864.06
Child 6	2 months	267.51	535.02	4 months	2,303.58	9,214.33		9,749.35

1. Based on the costs calculated in Holmes, McDermid and Sempik 2010, inflated for financial year 2010-11

and allowances. The costs for Child 6 also include the social care costs to obtain a Care Order (LAC Process 7).

The table shows that the average monthly costs for the children are notably higher once they become looked after. The timeline for Ruby included in Chapter 2 provides a detailed example of one of these children who became looked after. The timeline along with the data outlined in Table 6.3 demonstrate how extending the methodology to include children in need enables the costs of full care pathways of children with the greatest needs to be calculated.

While it was possible to calculate the costs across both the looked after children and children in need systems for six children, there were a further 15 children in the study sample for whom it was not clear whether they were looked after or children in need. The ability to identify more accurately the status of children as either in need or looked after would facilitate more effective cost calculations. Consequently, local authorities could more effectively cost children's full care trajectories and link these costs to outcomes. Improved data recording would increase the ability to examine the costs and effectiveness of services provided to those children with the greatest levels of need, and would ensure that finite resources were most effectively deployed.

Exploration of thresholds across authorities was carried out as part of the research to cost services to all children in need. Documentation from all of the authorities defined thresholds in terms of tiers or levels related to the dimensions of the Framework for the Assessment of Children in Need and their Families (Department of Health, Department for Education and Employment and The Home Office 2000). The decision to assess needs for the provision of service was determined by the tier or level of need identified in the Initial contact or referral. An examination of the different levels or tiers of need that informed the thresholds demonstrated complex variations: some of the authorities referred to level one as being the lowest level of need – often referred to as 'Children with no Additional Needs', others reversed this and used level one as the highest level of need and level three as the lowest. The latter (level three) was described as pre-social care involvement. Furthermore, the documentation illustrated differences between authorities in the number of tiers that they use. For example, some identified five tiers of needs while others only categorised needs according to three or four tiers. Another of the authorities had developed its own classification: the 'Common Assessment Thresholds of Needs and Interventions'. The latter was accompanied by a detailed flow diagram of the processes to 'ensure children and young people do not fall between these services'. It was based on a three level model, but levels were then split into seven separate subdivisions and pictorially presented as a pyramid with universal services at the base.

The use of differing models of thresholds and tiers for intervention makes comparison between authorities difficult. These differing approaches also exacerbate confusion around thresholds between agencies (Holmes, Munro and Soper 2010). Research has shown that social workers tend to operate higher thresholds than other professionals across partner agencies, for example education, health, housing and the police (see Ward *et al.* 2004). Furthermore, The National Foundation for Educational Research (Wilkin *et al.* 2008) has highlighted that social workers tend to have a higher threshold than teachers, and this can cause some tension, particularly where social workers are based in schools. Medical staff also perceive social workers to have higher thresholds, with the result that they may appear reluctant to intervene (Datta and Hart 2007). This evidence indicates that consistent thresholds are not yet uniformly accepted despite the production of 'universal' threshold policies. The last Joint Chief Inspectors report into the safeguarding of children (Commission for Social Care Inspection 2005) also highlighted concerns about the thresholds applied by children's social care and about the level of understanding of them by other agencies. The lack of clarity over the different tiers of services across and between localities is likely to increase the confusion and add to such concerns as agencies move towards greater integration. Emerging findings from the study to explore the costs and impact of CAF suggest that some agencies within some local authorities are unclear about when a case should be considered for social care intervention and when support under the auspices of CAF would be suitable (Holmes, McDermid and Padley forthcoming). Such confusion over thresholds may cause delays in the provision of suitable services and may increase costs over all.

Interpretations of thresholds may also have been affected by increased anxiety about safeguarding children. Brookes (2010) identified that there had been an increase of 20.3% in the number of section 47 Enquiries being undertaken, and a 32.9% increase in the number of children subject to a Child Protection Plan between 2007 and 2010. Staff levels, however, had only risen by 10%. Concerns have been expressed by practitioners and managers in a number of studies that due to the increased demand for services, and increasing pressure on social care teams, thresholds have been set so high that many families with considerable needs are not being given adequate support or access to necessary services (Sheppard 2008a; Sheppard 2008b; Holmes, Munro and Soper 2010). It is possible that some such cases may instead be managed under the auspices of CAF and some practitioners across child welfare agencies, other than social care have raised concerns about their ability to suitably meet the needs of these children and families (Holmes, McDermid and Padley forthcoming). As noted above, delays in providing appropriate timely intervention may result in needs increasing and requiring more costly services at a later date (Ward, Holmes and Soper 2008; Ward *et al.* 2010)

As noted in Chapter 3, where referrals do not meet social care thresholds additional activities are undertaken by social care referral and assessment team personnel to discuss the case with the referrer and this activity incurs a cost. These findings support those found elsewhere, that further training may be required to support practitioners across other agencies to undertake assessments such as CAF, and to develop a clearer understanding about the thresholds for social care intervention (Gilligan and Manby 2008; Ward *et al.* 2008 Norgate, Triall and Osborne 2009; Easton, Morris and Gee 2010).

The issue of confusion about when to refer a case to social care is highlighted by the cost case study for Jasmine who had multiple referrals to social care within a twelve month timeframe before she was deemed to meet the threshold for social care intervention.

Box 6.1 Jasmine's story

Jasmine was referred to social care at the age of three, two weeks into the data collection time frame, amid concerns about her parents' capacity to appropriately care for her. In the 12 months prior to the data collection time frame the family had been referred to social care three times. On each of these occasions it was deemed that the family's need was not sufficient to meet social care thresholds for intervention.

A Child in Need Plan was put in place for Jasmine following an Initial Assessment in October 2008. After increasing concerns about her parents' capacity for change, a section 47 Enquiry was completed and the child became subject to a Child Protection Plan from early December of the same year. In addition to ongoing support from the social worker, the family were offered a six week focussed piece of work on routine, delivered by the local authority's family support service.

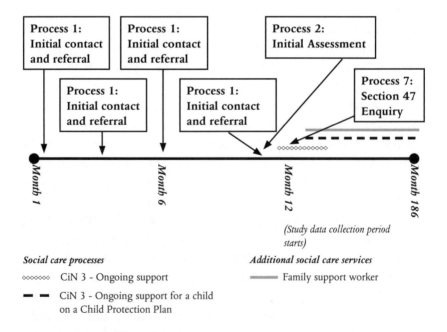

FIGURE 6.3 Timeline for Jasmine

TABLE 6.7: Costs incurred for a child with multiple referrals[1]

SOCIAL CARE ACTIVITY COSTS: OUT OF LONDON COSTS				ADDITIONAL SERVICES COSTS: OUT OF LONDON COSTS[2]			
				Social Care services			
Process	Frequency	Unit cost (£)	Sub total (£)	Service	Frequency	Unit cost (£)	Sub total (£)
CiN 1 - Initial contact and referral - No further action	3	213.19	639.58	Family Support worker	A one hour visit once a week for six weeks[3]	34.54	207.27
CiN 1 - Initial contact and referral		191.66	191.66				
CiN 2 - Initial Assessment		278.89	278.89				
CiN 3 - ongoing support (CiN)	1.5 months	192.70	289.05				
CiN 7 - section 47 enquiry		525.76	525.76				
CiN 3 - ongoing support (CP)	4.5 months	271.31	1,220.87				
Cost of social care case management activity (£)			3,145.81	Cost of service provision (£)			201.29
Total cost incurred by children's social care for Jasmine prior to the data collection period							£639.58
Total cost incurred by children's social care for Jasmine during the 6 month period							£5,652.04

1. Costs inflated for financial year 2010-11
2. There was no evidence of additional support services being provided by other agencies during the study timeframe
3. 'Bottom up' cost based on a one hour visit and 40 minutes travel time

In addition to the social care costs outlined above, it is possible that additional work may be have been carried out with Jasmine and her family under the auspices of the CAF before the case was allocated to social care. At the time of writing the case management processes for CAF are being drafted (see also Table 2.2) and costs of CAF are being calculated. Once these are available it will be possible to include these calculations to explore any additional costs incurred due to delays in decision making (Holmes, McDermid and Padley forthcoming).

The 2010 edition of *Working Together to Safeguard Children* (Department for Children, Schools and Families 2010) has been revised to clarify the statutory guidance on the interface between the Common Assessment Framework and the Assessment Framework for children in need and their families and threshold guidance. The unit costs of the CAF are as yet unknown, however, Holmes, Munro and Soper argue that:

> 'It may be beneficial for authorities to consider whether they could make efficiency savings [by] promoting more effective use of the CAF to reduce the time [social] workers are spending on ['front door' services, contacts and referrals] thereby freeing up more time to respond to 'appropriate' referrals and undertaking necessary assessments.' (2010: 48)

As previously discussed in this book, earlier research undertaken by CCFR suggests that a shift in policy focus towards preventative interventions, consolidated by the implementation of CAF, has resulted in a blurring of the boundaries between work that is undertaken specifically with children identified as being in need as defined by section 17 of the Children Act, and those receiving universal service provision, operating under a preventative agenda (Holmes, Munro and Soper 2010; Holmes, McDermid and Sempik 2010; Ward *et al.* 2008). Strategic managers participating in the study to cost all interventions to children in need reported that they would benefit from a better understanding of the numbers of families receiving support under CAF to build a more comprehensive understanding of the numbers of families receiving services and to ensure that services can be planned to meet local need.

As discussed in Chapter 4, at present there is no universal or systematic system for recording CAFs, and emerging findings suggest that the number of CAFs being undertaken within localities may be underestimated. This may be rectified by the introduction of National eCAF, a management information system for recording CAF which, at the time of writing, is being piloted across local authorities (Department for Education 2011d). Furthermore, evidence suggests that practitioners are reticent to undertake a CAF due to concerns about their own capacity and how the CAF process may impact their caseload (Norgate *et al.* 2009; Gillian and Manby 2008). Research is currently being undertaken to explore the costs and impact of CAF (Holmes, McDermid and Padley forthcoming). It is anticipated that the evidence from this study will allow for comparative cost calculations to be carried out across systems to support looked after children, children in need and those in receipt of a CAF assessment. Being able to follow a child's journey from identification of the need for *additional services*, prior to social care involvement, will add to the evidence base to understand the cost effectiveness of early intervention and preventative services.

Chapter 6: Summary

- Case study examples and cost timelines provide examples of how costs can be examined for individual children, and the relationship between children's needs, their circumstances and costs can be explored.

- Aggregated costs provide an evidence base for the strategic planning and commissioning of services for groups of children with specific needs, or for whole populations of children, for example looked after children, or children in need.

- The research team has developed a decision analysis tool to facilitate the calculations and to bring together all the different types of data outlined in the previous chapters (unit costs of *case management activities*; child level data outlining children's needs, circumstances, outcomes and social care support and assessments; data on *additional services*).

- Costs for children in need are increased when there are multiple referrals prior to them being considered to meet the threshold for social care intervention.

- There is a blurring of thresholds and an understanding of when children are deemed to meet the threshold for social care intervention. The methodology outlined in this book contributes to the evidence base to better understand the costs of providing support and services to these children and to better understanding the cost effectiveness of early intervention and preventative services.

CHAPTER 7

Conclusion

Implications for Policy and Practice

Introduction

This book describes a methodology for calculating unit costs of services provided to vulnerable children and brings together findings from a range of studies that have been carried out by the Centre for Child and Family Research. The studies form part of a wider research programme that aims to introduce comparability and transparency into the area of costing children's social care. The ultimate objective of the research is to make it possible for agencies to calculate and compare the full costs of providing services to vulnerable children, with a range of needs and to explore the relationship with outcomes.

This chapter brings together the key findings from the various research studies outlined in this book and examines their implications for policy and practice. Potential future extensions to the programme of research are also discussed.

Key findings from the research

Costing methodology

The various studies have used the unit costs of social care activity and support services as the basis of building up costs over time. The research has identified two different types of activity: *case management activity*, whereby a social care professional manages and supports the day to day needs of a case and *additional services* for vulnerable children and their families, including groups, parenting classes, or sessions aimed at addressing specific needs. These *additional services* may be provided either by the same team as those performing 'ongoing support' activities or by another team or agency.

Variations in costs

Previous research has shown that variations in costs are as a result of different needs or circumstances of children, differing types of provision and different local authority procedures (Ward, Holmes and Soper 2008). The research has highlighted that defining and recording the range of needs presented by children in need (including disabled children) and the variations in activity and costs is a complex issue. Frontline practitioners participating across a number of studies emphasised the necessity to view each case on an individual basis. They could not easily assign variations in activity in the provision of ongoing support for different types of cases. This was partly due to the complexity and variety of cases, but also because of the resilience of different families to cope with a range of difficulties and the changing nature of needs over time. Workers also noted that the categories of need used in the CiN Census were sufficient for the recording of cases, but did not reflect the complex needs of the children and families they were supporting.

Analysis of the data collected from case records and chronologies for the study to extend the costs to all children in need identified some variations in activity. Increased activity was identified for children under six, those who were subject to a Child Protection Plan or had emotional or behavioural difficulties. Use could be made of this data to categorise children and to calculate costs according to these needs groups.

Data recording and availability

The cost calculations have been carried out utilising routinely collected nationally applicable child level data. The decision analysis model developed by the team (outlined in Chapter 6) uses this data to identify when processes have occurred and any characteristics that can be linked to cost variations. The looked after version of the model utilises data gathered from the SSDA 903 national return (Department for Children, Schools and Families, 2009b) along with dates and financial information pertaining to fees and allowance payments for placements. As outlined in Chapter 5 the data for looked after children are more readily available and reliable than for other children in receipt of support or services provided by social care (Gatehouse, Ward and Holmes 2008). However, the research team have been able to make use of data collected for the revised CiN Census that was introduced in 2008. While authorities reported some difficulties with the newly introduced revised CiN Census, whereby they were having to back date data items for many of the children in their case loads.

The children in need study also highlighted a need to utilise supplementary data in addition to that collected for the CiN Census in order to fully understand all the activity to support children in need. The supplementary data was gathered manually from a range of sources, including assessments, minutes of meetings and other free text fields such as diary records.

The research has also identified variability in the reporting of *additional services*. The CiN Census requires the start and end date, service type and service provider to be recorded. This may be sufficient for accurate cost modelling of the *additional services* provided to children in need. However, the research found that in the first year of submission, local authorities experienced some difficulties in gathering data for *additional services*. These difficulties included the time consuming task of back dating service provision for the first round of data collection, applying the broad service types to the sheer range of service offered to children in need and electronically extracting data recorded in a number of different sources within management information systems. It is likely that as the CiN Census return develops, and as local authorities build up a historical dataset, the availability and quality of data on children in need will improve. As such future cost estimates of proving services to children in need will improve.

Implications for policy and practice

Analysis of need

There is evidence that a thorough analysis of the needs of children and their families is essential for the effective planning and commissioning of services. Children's needs not only impact on the type of *additional services* that might be accessed by them, but also on the type and level of *case management activities* they may require from social workers and from other frontline practitioners.

Evidence from the studies reported in this book suggest that the needs of children being referred to social care are becoming more complex, with the numbers of referrals and Child Protection Enquiries also increasing. Development of a comprehensive understanding of both the needs of children and how those needs impact on the workloads of frontline staff will be essential in the effective deployment of resources. An increase in knowledge of the complexity of needs would enable commissioners and service managers including those offering case management services, to tailor services and thereby maximise effectiveness.

As outlined in Chapter 5 the study to cost short break services highlighted that the level of assessment required for families was generally commensurate with the level of presenting need. However, the research also identified that this was not the case for children and families in receipt of direct payments (see case study examples in Chapter 6). Those families that had opted for direct payments as opposed to the 'local core offer model' were subject to additional assessments and *case management activities*, thereby providing an example of processes and assessment not being led by the needs of the child and their family.

Recording and analysis of data for practice development

Many criticisms have been made of the bureaucratisation of social work, the level of recording (McDermid 2008; Broadhurst *et al.* 2009; Holmes *et al.* 2009; Munro 2011) and the impact of new public management within the children's workforce (Munro 2010a; Burton and van den Broek 2008). As outlined in Chapter 5 some commentators have noted that the increased burden on social workers and other professionals to provide evidence for national returns has created a 'tick box' culture, which is over-reliant on processes and meeting targets (Munro 2011b). However, while it is essential to ensure that the burden of collecting evidence does not prevent frontline workers from carrying out their core business of supporting families, the data recorded by practitioners can be used to support both policy and practice and provide an evidence base for decision making.

Previous research suggests that the most effective use of data can be found where both practitioners and managers develop a learning culture in which the ability and willingness to use data to inform practice and planning is encouraged (McDermid 2008; Scott, Moore and Ward 2005). In a system where the majority of data is recorded in management information systems by frontline practitioners, rather than performance managers, the frontline practitioners need to be able to link the data they are recording to their own practice, and utilise the data for future enhancements to their practice. Gatehouse and Ward (2003) note that increasingly, performance management staff are being employed within local authorities to assist in the collection of data for national returns. This may be creating a division between those who record the data (the practitioners) and use who use it (performance and commissioning managers). Furthermore, Scott, Moore and Ward (2003) argue that the quality of data recording is likely to be improved where those entering the data, in this case practitioners, are able to see the benefits of recording. Therefore, the best quality data and therefore, a more robust evidence base can be achieved where an organisational culture is nurtured which links these two groups; where practitioners understand the uses of child level data, and are enabled to use the data to inform service provision and their own practice.

As noted in Chapter 3, recent concerns have been raised about the amount of time spent by front line workers to input data into management information systems: time which may otherwise be spent working directly with families. While the collection of data is informative for planning and practice, the efforts to collect data should not be greater that the value gained from analysing it. As Chapter 3 notes, some *case management activities* have a higher administrative component than others and some reported figures may overestimate the time spent on administrative tasks. However, barriers to data collection may arise due to challenges faced by local authorities and software developers to design management information systems that both reflect the needs of those inputting the data and that produce appropriate outputs. In a number of studies carried out by CCFR, workers reported that management information systems are difficult to navigate and do not always sufficiently reflect practice (McDermid 2008; Holmes *et al.* 2009; Holmes *et al.* 2010; Holmes, Munro and Soper 2010). Frontline workers also reported that they are constrained by categories defined by fields in management information system and in many cases social workers utilise free text fields to ensure the information is being recorded (McDermid 2008). Free text data can be useful in creating a narrative of a child or family's circumstances, which is essential for everyday case work. It is however, prohibitively time consuming to gather for monitoring and analysis purposes. As noted by McDermid (2008), tensions arise when developing a recording system that both facilitates systematic, routine collection of data for use in system analysis, such as the calculation of costs, and reflects the varied and complex nature of work carried out with vulnerable children. Scott, Moore and Ward (2005) observe that many information systems have been designed to store and record data with little attention being given as to how they might be used to support practice or decision making.

Furthermore, recent policy has emphasised the need for de-centralisation and a less prescriptive approach from national government to implementing services. This will enable local authorities to develop services and models of delivery that are designed specifically to meet local need. In addition, it is likely that local data collections will also be developed. Emerging findings from the research to explore the costs and impact of the Common Assessment Framework (CAF), suggest that, in the case of CAF, the nature, availability and quality of data gathered about families receiving support under the auspices of CAF may vary considerable between local authorities. This may reduce the possibility of obtaining comparable data sets and undertaking analysis of both the cost and effectiveness of interventions and services across localities or at a national level. UK child level data collections, including the Children in Need (CiN) Census, are internationally recognised as being robust and providing valuable national longitudinal data on a number of key variables (Munro *et al.* 2011a).

The value of child level data lies primarily in its ability to provide detailed information on each aspect of supporting a child. The decision analysis tool has demonstrated that much can be gained by using this data to calculate costs for different types of children, receiving different service packages over time. However, this requires management information systems to be designed in such a way as to reflect the needs of both practitioners and commissioners and where the burden of inputting data is not greater than the benefits gained from it. The children's workforce, at all levels, will make little use of child level data unless it can be seen to produce sufficient dividends to warrant the effort of collection.

Taking a systems approach

This book has highlighted the need for a comprehensive understanding of the costs incurred to support children and families. The findings also demonstrate the need to take a systems approach to cost calculations, whereby the impact of changes to one area of service provision on another service area is understood. The importance of understanding a child's journey as they receive support from a range of services in response to specific needs has recently been highlighted as part of the Munro *Review of Child Protection* (Munro 2010; Munro 2011a). The costs and outcomes programme of research at CCFR has, in part, developed due to a recognition of the need for a systems approach to cost calculations. In the original study to explore the costs of placing children in care, Ward, Holmes and Soper (2008) note that:

> 'The costs incurred by placing children in care or accommodation should be considered within the context of the costs of providing targeted services to all children in need – and against the wider background of providing universal services to all children within an authority' (p.256)

The inclusion of children in need (Holmes *et al.* 2010), children with disabilities (Holmes, McDermid and Sempik 2010), children with special educational needs (Homes *et al.* forthcoming) and children in receipt of specialist interventions (Holmes, Westlake and Ward 2008) have facilitated an increase in the understanding of the costs of support provided to all vulnerable children and their families. Ward, Holmes and Soper (2008) highlight the importance of understanding the impact on costs across agencies when there is a change in a child's circumstances. For instance, the original study identified that young people who were excluded from school were also more likely to offend, so a reduction in costs to education may increase costs to youth offending teams.

Recent policy and practice developments, as noted in Chapter 1, have made the need for such an approach increasingly pertinent. While children have long since received services from a number of different agencies and providers, moves towards both a more integrated approach to service provision and great utilisation of the independent sector to provide services has created a labyrinthine map of service provision for vulnerable children and families (Ward *et al.* 2008). Numerous service delivery and commissioning arrangements with jointly commissioned services provided by the independent sector, along with multi-agency and co-located teams, are now in place across various local authorities. In addition to joint service provision, *case management activities*, such as assessments are increasingly becoming multi-agency. While assessments have long since been carried out in consultation with all professionals working with a child (Ward and Rose 2002) new assessments such as the Common Assessment Framework (Children's Workforce Development Council 2009) and the Education, Health and Care Plan for children with disabilities and special needs (Department for Education 2011c) are designed to cement a multi-agency approach to both assessing the needs of children and families and delivering the services intended to meet those need. Consequently, the onus on practitioners, planners and policy makers to understand a broader picture of the costs incurred by supporting vulnerable children and families has increased.

A systems approach can shed light on both the costs of a service and its impact. For instance, Ward, Holmes and Soper (2008) note that increasing the level of provision from child and adolescent mental health services (and therefore the costs to the Health service), may reduce the costs to social care if young people with emotional or behavioural difficulties are better supported at home, with their families. Furthermore, emerging findings from the study to explore the costs and impact of CAF suggest that despite substantive investment in the CAF processes (for example assessment, support and review), notable cuts to the services that would otherwise be provided to meet the needs identified in the CAF assessment, is undermining the CAF process (Holmes, McDermid and Padley forthcoming). The services that would have previously supported families subject to a CAF assessment have either been reduced substantially or are no longer in place.

Invest to save: Early intervention and prevention

The research reported in this book demonstrates the importance of understanding costs over time, particularly how care journeys build up. Many children have complex care trajectories, moving in and out of care, or in and out of social care thresholds for intervention. While empirical analysis of the impact of early intervention strategies is complex, there is some evidence to suggest that providing services earlier will reduce the need for more intensive services at a later stage (Beresford 1994; Chan and Sigafoos 2001; Farrington and Welsh 2004; Axford and Little 2006; Allen 2011b). Allen (2011b) notes that:

> 'People who have adverse early childhood experiences can end up costing society millions of pounds through their lifetimes, both in direct spending to cope with their problems and behaviours and in the indirect loss of output and tax revenues from themselves and those they affect.' (p.24)

Allen (2011b) notes that at a time of economic austerity, investment in early intervention strategies are vital to ensure the sustainability of services for vulnerable children and families and can provide high levels of social return on investment.

Planned enhancements and future research

The original study was restricted to explore the costs and outcomes for looked after children. However, it was always recognised that the services that looked after children receive are part of a continuum, and therefore this led to the research to extend the methodology for all children in need. This book has reported the findings from a number of studies, related in their methodology and approach to understanding the costs of services provided to vulnerable children.

The ongoing research programme continues to build on all these studies and to try to replicate the methodology across a range of service areas and to understand the costs incurred by a range of agencies, and thereby work towards the overall aim of being able to determine the costs to the public purse of providing services to vulnerable children.

One of the key advantages of the methodology that has been outlined in this book is the ability to introduce transparency and comparability into cost calculations. The research team are now starting a new study to compare the costs of services provided by local authorities and the voluntary sector. The focus of this new study is short break services for disabled children, it is anticipated that one of the outputs from the research will be a framework for cost comparisons across providers that can then be piloted and replicated across a wider range of child welfare service areas, for example foster care providers (McDermid and Holmes forthcoming).

Some of the emerging findings from the study to explore the costs and impact of the Common Assessment Framework have been reported, further work is currently underway to explore the data availability on CAF assessments and how the data in the participating authorities can potentially be linked with that for children in need and looked after children already utilised in the decision analysis tool (outlined in the previous chapter). Interviews with families in receipt of support under CAF arrangements will provide additional data about service receipt and also outcomes (Holmes, McDermid and Padley forthcoming).

Work is also currently underway to replicate the methodology for the child welfare system in the US, facilitating international comparisons (Chamberlain *et al.* 2010).

Although the research programme has developed in such a way to explore earlier intervention and preventative services, the research team acknowledge the need to understand the longer term outcomes and as such ways of being able to measure and record longer term wellbeing outcomes (see Holder, Beecham and Knapp 2011 for further information about the development of a wellbeing outcome measure for children's services).

Conclusion

It is evident from the research programme, that the provision of services for vulnerable children and their families is a highly complex area, undergoing continued policy and practice change. Children's services departments are experiencing increasing workloads, while financial resources are under sustained pressure. The studies outlined in this book illustrate how child level data can be utilised to calculate the costs of *case management activities*, and how this can be aggregated in various ways to inform decision making. As social work teams experience increased workloads, the methodology and analysis contribute to an evidence base which can assist service managers in understanding how finite resources might be most usefully deployed to ensure that all children receive services that are appropriate to their needs.

It is apparent that there is a need for a transparent and comprehensive costing methodology that, in a time of economic austerity, can assist local authorities and other agencies in examining how finite resources can be most effectively deployed in order to provide support to the most vulnerable and to ensure that all children achieve positive outcomes.

Chapter 7: Summary

- The unit costing methodology originally developed for looked after children can be replicated and extended across a range of service areas.

- Defining and recording the range of needs presented by vulnerable children and their families is complex.

- Use can be made of nationally applicable routinely collected data sets. As these datasets improve and are built up over the years to create historical datasets, then cost calculations and estimates can be improved.

- The quality of data recorded on local authority management information systems is likely to be improved if the data and analysis of that data can be linked back to frontline practice.

- The research findings demonstrate the importance of adopting a systems approach to analysing costs of providing services to vulnerable children. To explore costs across different social care service areas and also examine how costs are spread across agencies.

References

Action for Children (2011) *The Red Book: Impact of UK Government Spending Decisions on Children, Young People and Families 2010/11.* Watford: Action for Children.

Alexander, D. (2010) Speech to the Inverness Chamber of Commerce 27 August 2010. Available at http://www.hm-treasury.gov.uk/speech_cst_270810.htm, accessed 3/9/10.

Allen, G. (2011a) *Early Intervention: The Next Steps.* London: HM Government.

Allen, G. (2011b) *Early Intervention: Smart Investment, Massive Savings* London: HM Government.

Atkinson Review (2005) *Measurement of Government Output and Productivity the National Accounts Final Report.* Hampshire: Palgrave MacMillan.

Audit Commission (2002) *Recruitment and Retention: A Public Service Workforce for the 21st Century.* London: Audit Commission.

Axford, N., Green, V., Kalsbeek, A., Morpeth, L. and Palmer, C. (2009) 'Measuring Children's Needs: How are we doing?' *Child and Family Social Work 14,*3, 243–254.

Axford, N. and Little, M. (2006) 'Refocusing children's services towards prevention: Lessons from the literature.' *Children and Society 20,* 299 – 312.

Baginsky, M., Moriarty, J., Manthorpe, J., Stevens, M., MacInnes, T. and Nagendran, T. (2010) *Messages from the Frontline: Findings from the Social Workers' Workload Survey and Interviews with Senior Managers.* Leeds: Children's Workforce Development Council.

Becker, S. and Bryman, A. (2004) *Understanding Research for Social Policy and Practice: Themes, Methods and Approaches.* Bristol: The Policy Press.

Beecham, J. (2000) *Unit Costs – Not Exactly Child's Play: A Guide to Estimating Unit Costs for Children's Social Care.* University of Kent: Department of Health, Dartington Social Research Unit and the Personal Social Services Research Unit.

Beecham, J. and Knapp, M. (2001) 'Costing psychiatric interventions.' In G.Thornicroft (ed.) *Measuring Mental Health Needs – 2nd edition.* London: Gaskell, 200-224.

Beecham, J. and Sinclair, I. (2007) *Costs and Outcomes in Children's Social Care.* London: Jessica Kingsley Publishers.

Bell, M., Shaw, I., Sinclair, I., Sloper, P. and Rafferty, J. (2007) *The Integrated Children's System: An Evaluation of the Practice, Process and Consequences of the ICS in Councils with Social Services Responsibilities.* York: Department of Social Policy and Social Work, University of York.

Beresford, B. (1994) 'Resources and strategies: How parents cope with the care of a disabled child.' *Journal of Child Psychology and Psychiatry 35,* 171–209.

Broadhurst, K., Wastell, D., White, S., Hall, C., Peckover, S., Thompson, K., Pithouse, A. and Davey, D. (2009) 'Performing 'initial assessment': identifying the latent conditions for error at the front-door of local authority children's services.' *British Journal of Social Work,* Advanced access online; published 18th January 2009.

Brookes, C. (2010) *Safeguarding Pressures Projects: Results of Data Collection.* London: Association of Directors of Children's Services.

Burton, J. and van den Broek, D. (2008) 'Accountable and countable: information management systems and bureaucratization of social work.' *British Journal of Social Work 37,* 7, 1326–1342.

Byford, S. and Fiander, M. (2007) 'Recording professional activities to aid economic evaluations of health and social care services.' In L. Curtis (ed) *The Unit Costs of Health and Social Care 2007.* Kent: Personal Social Services Research Unit, University of Kent.

Cabinet Office (2011) *Open Public Services: White paper.* London: HMSO.

Carlin, J. and Cramer, H. (2007) *Creative Responses to Changing Needs? Fourth National Survey of Short Break Services for Disabled Children in the UK.* Bristol: Shared Care Network.

Chamberlain, P., Snowden, L.R., Padgett, C., Saldana, L., Roles, J., Holmes, L.J., Ward, H., Reid, J. and Landsverk, J. (2010) A Strategy for Assessing Costs of Implementing New Practices in the Child Welfare System: Adapting the English Cost Calculator in the United States. *Children and Youth Services Review.*

Chan, J. and Sigafoos, J. (2001) 'Does respite care reduce parent stress in families with developmentally disabled children?' *Children and Youth Care Forum 30,* 253–263.

Children Act (1989) London: Her Majesty's Stationary Office.

Children Act (2004) London: Her Majesty's Stationary Office.

Children's Workforce Development Council (2009) *The Common Assessment Framework for Children and Young People: A Guide for Practitioners.* Leeds: Children's Workforce Development Council.

Cleaver, H., Walker, S. and Meadows, P. (2004) *Assessing Children's Needs and Circumstances.* London: Jessica Kingsley Publishers.

Cm 7589 (2009) *The Protection of Children in England: Action Plan. The Government's response to Lord Laming.* London: Department for Children, Schools and Families.

Commission for Social Care Inspection (2005) *Safeguarding Children: The Second Joint Chief Inspectors Report on Arrangements to Safeguard Children.* London: CSCI.

Community Care Online 04.10.2007, available at http://www.communitycare.co.uk/Articles/2007/10/04/105987/cutting-the-red-tape-moves-toslash-social-workers-paperwork.html.

Corby, B. (2006) 'The role of child care social work in supporting families with children in need and providing protective services – past present and future.' *Child abuse review 15,* 3, 159–177.

Curtis, L. (ed) (2007) *The Unit Costs of Health and Social Care 2007.* Kent: Personal Social Services Research Unit, University of Kent.

Curtis, L. (ed) (2010) *The Unit Costs of Health and Social Care 2010.* Kent: Personal Social Services Research Unit, University of Kent.

Curtis, L. (ed) (forthcoming) *The Unit Costs of Health and Social Care 2011.* Kent: Personal Social Services Research Unit, University of Kent.

Datta, J. and Hart, D. (2007) *A Shared Responsibility; Safeguarding Arrangements between Hospitals and Children's Social Services.* London: National Children's Bureau. Available at http://www.ncb.org.uk/dotpdf/open_access_2/hossi_final_report_march07.pdf, accessed 28/02/08.

Deacon, A. (2002) *Perspectives on Welfare.* Buckinghamshire: Open University Press.

Department for Children, Schools and Families (2007*) The Common Assessment Framework for Children and Young People. A Guide for Managers.* London: Department for Children, Schools and Families.

Department for Children, Schools and Families (2008) *Aiming High for Disabled Children: Short Breaks Implementation Guidance.* London: Department for Children's Schools and Families.

Department for Children, Schools and Families (2009) *Guidance Notes for the Completion of the Children in Need Census.* London: Departments for Children Schools and Families.

Department for Children, Schools and Families (2010) *Working Together to Safeguard Children: A Guide to Inter-agency Working to Safeguard and Promote the Welfare of Children.* London: Department for Children Schools and Families.

Department for Education (2010a) *Children Assessed to be In Need by Children's Social Services, England, 6 Months Ending 31 March 2010.* London: Department for Education.

Department for Education (2010b) *Children Looked After in England (including adoption and care leavers) Year Ending 31st March 2010).* London: Department for Education.

Department for Education (2010c) *Serious Case Review 'Child A' November 2008.* London: Department for Education.

Department for Education (2010d) *Serious Case Review 'Child A' March 2009.* London: Department for Education.

Department for Education (2010e) *Financial Reports on Local Authority Planned Budgets for their Education and Children's Social Care Functions: 2010–11 (section 251 formerly s52)* London: Department for Education.

Department for Education (2011a) *A Child Centred System: The Government's Response to the Munro Review, July 2011.* London: Department for Education.

Department for Education (2011b) *Short Breaks for Carers of Disabled Children: Advice for Local Authorities.* London: Department for Education.

Department for Education (2011c) *Support and Aspiration: A New Approach to Special Educational Needs and Disability: Green Paper.* London: Department for Education.

Department for Education (2011d) *National eCAF 0* Available at http://www.education.gov.uk/childrenandyoungpeople/strategy/integratedworking/caf/a0072820/national-ecaf, accessed 08/03/11.

Department for Education and Skills (2004) *Every Child Matters: Change for Children*. London: Department for Education and Skills.

Department for Education and Skills (2005) *Children in Need in England: Results of a Survey of Activity and Expenditure as Reported by Local Authority Social Services' Children and Families Teams for a Survey Week in February 2005*. London: Department for Education and Skills.

Department for Education and Skills (2007) *Care Matters: Time for Change*. London: Department for Education and Skills.

Department of Health (1989) *An Introduction to the Children Act 1989*. London: HMSO.

Department of Health (1995) *Messages from Research: Studies in Child Protection*. London: Her Majesty's Stationary Office.

Department of Health (2000) *The Quality Protects Programme: Transforming Children's Services 2001-02 (LAC (2000)22)*. London: Department of Health.

Department of Health (2001a) *Core Requirements Process Model*. London: Department of Health.

Department of Health (2001b) *Children in Need in England: Results of a Survey of Activity and Expenditure as Reported by Local Authority Social Services Children and Families Teams for a Survey Week in February 2000*. London: Department of Health.

Department of Health (2002) *National Minimum Standards for Children's Homes: Children's Homes Regulations*. London: The Stationery Office.

Department of Health (2003) *Direct Payments Guidance: Community Care, Services for Carers and Children's Services (Direct Payments) Guidance*. London: Department of Health.

Department of Health, Department for Education and Employment and Home Office (2000) *Framework for the Assessment of Children in Need and their Families*. London: The Stationery Office.

Dewson, S., Eccles, J., Tackey, N.D. and Jackson, A. (2000) *Guide to Measuring Soft Outcomes and Distance Travelled*. Brighton: Institute for Education.

Dobson, B. (2004) 'Focus groups.' In S. Becker and A. Bryman (eds) *Understanding Research for Social Policy and Practice: Themes, Methods and Approaches*. Bristol: The Policy Press, 284–290.

Easton, C., Morris, M. and Gee, G. (2010) *LARC2: Integrated Children's Services and the CAF Process*. Slough: National Foundation for Educational Research.

Farrington, D. and Welsh, B. (2004) 'Economic costs and benefits of early intervention.' In S. Sutton, D. Utting and D. Farrington (eds) *Support from the Start: Working with Young Children and their Families to Reduce the Risks of Crime and Anti-social Behaviour Research report 524*. Nottingham: Department for Education and Skills.

Felton, K. (2005) 'Meaning based quality of life measurement: A way forward in conceptualising and measuring client outcomes?' *British Journal of Social Work 35*, 221–236.

Flynn, R. J., Dudding, P. and Barber, J. G. (2006) *Promoting Resilience in Child Welfare.* Ottawa: University of Ottawa Press.

France, A., Freiberg, K. and Homel, R. (2010) 'Beyond risk factors: Towards a holistic prevention paradigm for children and young people.' *British Journal of Social Work.* Advance access February 2010.

Garrett, P.M. (1999) 'Producing the moral citizen: The 'Looking After Children' system and the regulation of children and young people in public care.' *Critical Social Policy 19,* 291–311.

Garrett, P.M. (2003) 'Swimming with dolphins: The assessment framework, new labour and new tools for social work with children and families.' *British Journal of Social Work 33,* 3, 441–463.

Gatehouse, M., Ward, H. and Holmes, L. (2008) *Developing Definitions of Local Authority Services and Guidance for the New Children in Need Census, Final report to the Department for Children Schools and Families.* London: Department of Children, Schools and Families.

Gatehouse, M. and Ward, H. (2003) *Making Use of Information in Children's Social Services. Final Report to Wales Office of Research and Development for Health and Social Care.* Loughborough: Centre for Child and Family Research.

Gilligan, P. and Manby, M. (2008) 'The common assessment framework: Does the reality match the rhetoric?' *Child and Family Social Work 13,2,* 177–187.

Goodman R (1997) 'The Strengths and Difficulties Questionnaire: A Research Note.' *Journal of Child Psychology and Psychiatry,* 38, 581–586.

Henn, M., Weinstein M. and Foard, N. (2006) *A Short Introduction to Social Research.* London: Sage Publications.

Herbert, I. (2004) 'Pressure of paperwork stops social workers from working.' *The Independent Online,* 30.04.2004, available at http://www.independent.co.uk/

HM Treasury, Department for Education and Skills, Department of Work and Pensions, Department for Trade and Industry (2005) *Choice for Parents, The Best Start for Children: A Ten Year Strategy for Childcare.* Norwich: HMSO.

HM Treasury (2010) Spending Review Statement. H.M. Treasury. Available at http://www. hm-treasury.gov.uk/spend_sr2010_speech.htm, accessed 17th March 2011.

Holder, J., Beecham, J. and Knapp, E. (2011) *Developing a Wellbeing Outcome Measure for use in Economic Evaluations of Children's Services: Identifying Domains Important to Children and Young People.* London: Childhood Wellbeing Research Centre.

Holmes, L. and Jones, A. (forthcoming) *The Cost of Decision Making Panels.* Loughborough: Centre for Child and Family Research, Loughborough University.

Holmes, L., Lam, S.C., Ward, H. and Simpson, M. (forthcoming) *Special Educational Needs Processes: Their Cost and Variations.* Loughborough: Centre for Child and Family Research, Loughborough University.

Holmes, L., McDermid, S., Jones, A., Ward, H. (2009) *How Social Workers Spend Their Time: An Analysis of the Key Issues that Impact on Practice pre-and post implementation of the Children's Integrated System,* London: Department of Children, Schools and Families.

Holmes, L., McDermid, S. and Padley, M. (forthcoming) *An Exploration of the Costs and Impact of the Common Assessment Framework: Final Report to the Department for Education.* Loughborough: Centre for Child and Family Research, Loughborough University.

Holmes, L., McDermid, S. and Sempik, J. (2010) *The Costs of Short Break Provision.* London: Department for Children, Schools and Families.

Holmes, L., McDermid, S. and Sempik, J. (2011) *Exploration of the Costs and Impact of the Common Assessment Framework: Re-analysis of Child Level Data on Services Provided to Children in Need: Report to the Department for Education.* London: Department for Education.

Holmes, L., McDermid, S. and Soper, J. (2011) *An Exploration of the Costs and Impact of the Common Assessment Framework: Interim Report to the Department for Education* Loughborough: Centre for Child and Family Research, Loughborough University.

Holmes, L., McDermid, S., Soper, J., Sempik, J. and Ward, H. (2010) *Extension of the Cost Calculator to Include Cost Calculations for all Children in Need: Research Brief.* London: Department for Education.

Holmes, L., Munro, E.R. and Soper, J. (2010) *The Costs and Capacity Implications of Implementing Laming (2009) Recommendations.* Loughborough: Centre for Child and Family Research, Loughborough University.

Holmes, L., Sempik, J., and Soper, J. (2009) *Calculating Unit Costs for the Children's Continuing Care Framework: Report to the Department of Health.* Loughborough: Centre for Child and Family Research, Loughborough University.

Holmes, L., Westlake, D. and Ward, H. (2008) *Calculating and Comparing the Costs of Multidimensional Treatment Foster Care, England (MTFCE): Report to the Department for Children, Schools and Families.* Loughborough: Centre for Child and Family Research, Loughborough University.

HM Government (2006) *Working Together to Safeguard Children: A Guide to Inter-agency Working to Safeguard and Promote the Welfare of Children.* London: The Stationery Office.

Holmes, L.with Lawson, D. and Stone, J. (2005) *Looking after Children: At What Cost? Resource Pack.* London: Department for Education and Skills.

Janzon, K. and Sinclair, R. (2002) 'Needs, numbers, resources: Informed planning for looked after children. *Research Policy and Planning 20,*2,1–7.

Knapp, M., Bryson, D. and Lewis, J. (1984) *The comprehensive costing of child care: Suffolk cohort study.* PSSRU discussion paper 355. Canterbury: Personal Social Services Research Unit: University of Kent.

Laming, The Lord (2009) *The Protection of Children in England: A Progress Report.* London: The Stationery Office.

Mahon, J. (2008) *Towards the New Children in Need Census.* London: Department for Children, Schools and Families.

McCann, D. (2009) *Scoping Exercise into the Training and Induction Standards for the Short Breaks Workforce.* London: Shared Care Network.

McConkey, R., Truesdale, M. and Confliffe, C. (2004) 'The features of short break residential services valued by families who have children with multiple disabilities.' *Journal of Social Work 4,* 1, 61–75.

McDermid, S. (2008) 'The nature and availability of child level data on children in need for use by children's services practitioners and managers.' *Research, Policy and Planning 26,* 3, 183–192.

McDermid, S. (2010) *The Cost of Short Break Provision. Resource pack for Service Providers.* Loughborough: Centre for Child and Family Research, Loughborough University.

McDermid, S. and Holmes, L. (forthcoming) *Cost Comparisons of Action for Children Short Break Services.* Loughborough: Centre for Child and Family Research, Loughborough University.

McDermid, S., Soper, J., Lushey, C., Lawson, D. and Holmes, L. (2011) *Evaluation of the Impact of Action for Children Short Break Services on Outcomes for Children - Final Report: Report to Action for Children June 2011.* Loughborough: Centre for Child and Family Research, Loughborough University.

Millar, M. and Corby, B. (2006) 'The framework for the assessment of children in need and their families – a basis for a "therapeutic" encounter?'. *British Journal of Social Work. 36,* 6, 887–899.

Munro, E.R., Brown, R., Sempik, J. and Ward, H. with Owen, C. (2011a) *Scoping Review to Draw Together Data on Child Injury and Safeguarding and to Compare the Position of England with that in Other Countries, Report to the Department for Education.* Childhood Wellbeing Research Centre, Institute of Education, University of London, Centre for Child and Family Research, Loughborough University, PSSRU, University of Kent.

Munro, E.R., Ward, H., Lushey, C. and National Care Advisory Service (2011b) *Evaluation of the Right2BCared4 pilots final report.* Loughborough: Centre for Child and Family Research, Loughborough University.

Munro, E. (2004) 'The impact of audit on social work practice.' *British Journal of Social Work 34,* 8, 1075–1095.

Munro, E. (2010) *The Munro Review of Child Protection Part One: A Systems Analysis.* London: Department for Education.

Munro, E. (2011a) *The Munro Review of Child Protection Part One: Interim Report: The Child's Journey.* London: Department for Education.

Munro, E. (2011b) *The Munro Review of Child Protection Final report.* London: Department for Education.

Norgate, R., Traill, M. and Osbourne, C. (2009) Common Assessment Framework (CAF) – early views and issues. *Educational Psychology in Practice, 25,* 2,139–150.

Ofsted (2010) *The Special Educational Needs and Disability Review: A Statement is not Enough.* Manchester: Ofsted.

Percy-Smith, J. (1992) 'Auditing Social Needs.' *Policy and Politics 20,* 1, 29–34.

Preston-Shoot, M, and Wigley, V. (2005) 'Mapping the Needs of Children in Need.' *British Journal of Social Work 35,* 2, 255–275.

Prince's Trust (2007) *The Cost of Exclusion.* London: Prince's Trust. Available at http://www.princes-trust.org.uk/Main%20Site%20v2/search/search.idq, accessed 28/10/08.

Robertson, J., Hatton, C., Emerson, E., Wells, E., Collins, M., Langer, S. and Welch, V. (2010) *The Impacts of Short Break Provision on Disabled Children and Families: An International Literature Review.* London: Department for Children Schools and Families.

Robinson, C., Jackson, P. and Townsley, R. (2001) 'Short breaks for families caring for a disabled child with complex health needs.' *Child and Family Social Work 6,*1, 67–75.

Rowlands, J. (2011) Need, well-being and outcomes: The development of policy-thinking for children's services 1989–2004. *Child and Family Social Work 16,*3, 255–265.

Scott, J., Moore, T. and Ward, H. (2005) 'Evaluating Interventions and Monitoring Outcomes.' In J. Scott and H. Ward (eds.) *Safeguarding and Promoting the Well-being of Children, Families and Communities.* London: Jessica Kingsley Publishers, 262–273.

Selwyn, J., Sempik, J., Thurston, P. and Wijedasa, D. (2009*) Adoption and the Inter-agency Fee.* London: Department for Children, Schools and Families.

Seneviratna, C. (2007) 'Cutting the red tape: moves to slash social workers' paperwork.'

Shaw, I., Bell, M., Sinclair, I., Sloper, P., Mitchell, W., Dyson, P. and Rafferty, J. (2007) 'An exemplary scheme? An evaluation of the integrated children's system.' *British Journal of Social Work 39,* 613–626.

Sheppard, M. (2008a) High thresholds and prevention in children's services: The impact of mothers' coping strategies on outcome of child and parenting problems – six month follow up. *British Journal of Social Work 38,*7,1268–1282.

Sheppard, M. (2008b) How important is prevention? High thresholds and outcomes for applicants refused by Children's services: A six month follow up. *British Journal of Social Work 39,* 46–63.

Skuse, T. and Ward, H. (2003) *Outcomes for Looked After Children: Children's Views of Care and Accommodation. An interim report to the Department of Health.* Loughborough: Centre for Child and Family Research, Loughborough University.

Social Work Task Force (2009) *Building a Safe and Confident Future- The Final Report of the Social Work Taskforce.* London: Department for Children, Schools and Families.

Soper, J. (2007) Cost *Calculator for Children's Services, V6.0 Demonstration Version.* Loughborough: Centre for Child and Family Research, Loughborough University.

Soper, J., Holmes, L., Hu, X. and D'Souza, E. (2006) *Valuing Changes in Welfare to Individuals and Society Resulting from the Government's Provision of Children's Social Services in England. Report to the DfES.* London: Department for Education and Skills.

Statham, J. and Smith, M. (2010) *Issues in Earlier Intervention: Identifying and Supporting Children with Additional Needs.* London: Department for Children, Schools and Families.

Tidmarsh, J. and Schneider, J. (2005) 'Typical costs of Sure Start Local Programmes.' In L. Curtis (ed) *Unit Costs of Health and Social Care 2005.* Kent: Personal Social Services Research Unit, University of Kent.

UN General Assembly (2009) *Guidelines for the Alternative Care of Children Resolution GE.09-14213 (E) 160609.*

UNICEF/Better Care Network (2009) *Manual for the Measurement of Indicators for Children in Formal Care.* New York: UNICEF.

Wade, J., Biehal, N., Farrelly, N. and Sinclair, I. (2010) *Maltreated Children in the Looked After System: A Comparison of Outcomes for those Who Go Home and those Who Do Not, Research Brief,* DFE-RBX-10-06. London: Department for Education.

Ward, H., Brown, R., Westlake, D. and Munro, E.R. (forthcoming) Safeguarding Babies and Very Young Children from Abuse and Neglect. London: Jessica Kingsley Publishers.

Ward, H., Holmes, L., Dyson, P. and McDermid, S. (2008) *The Costs and Consequences of Child Welfare Interventions: Mapping Children in Need Services.* Loughborough: Centre for Child and Family Research, Loughborough University.

Ward, H., Holmes, L., Munro, E., Moyers, S. and Poursanidou, K. (2004) *Safeguarding Children: A Scoping Study of Research in Three Areas. Report to the Department for Education and Skills.* Loughborough: Centre for Child and Family Research, Loughborough University.

Ward, H., Holmes, L. and Soper, J. (2005) *CCFR Cost Calculator for Children's Services: the Pilot Phase. Report to Department for Education and Skills.* Loughborough: Centre for Child and Family Research, Loughborough University.

Ward, H., Holmes, L. and Soper, J. (2008) *Costs and Consequences of Placing Children in Care.* London: Jessica Kingsley Publishers.

Ward, H. and Jackson, J. (1991) 'Research note: Researching outcomes in child care.' *British Journal of Social Work 21*, 393–399.

Ward, H. and Rose, W. (2002) *Approaches to Needs Assessment in Children's Services.* London: Jessica Kingsley Publishers.

Wiggins, L. and Storry, R. (2010) *Slow Progress? A Review of Social Workers' Pay and Progression: A Report for Unison.* London: Income Data Services.

Wilkin, A., Murfield, J., Lamont, E., Kinder, K. and Dyson, P. (2008) *The Value of Social Care Professionals Working in Extended Schools.* Slough: National Foundation for Educational Research.

Wood, C., Cheetham, P., and Gregory, P. (2011) *Coping with the Cuts.* London: Demos.

Subject Index

Author Index